Designing and Building
Space-Saving
Furniture
with 28 Projects
2nd Edition

TAB FURNITURE WOODSHOP SERIES

Other Books in The TAB Furniture Woodshop Series

Do-It-Yourselfer's Guide to Furniture Repair and Refinishing—2nd Edition

Brush up on the latest woodworking techniques and applications.
Restore furniture to its original character and beauty—even make it better than it was! Precise directions cover everything from selecting a finish to using stains and fillers, from stripping the old varnish to applying the new, even restoring cane, metal, and bamboo furniture. Almost 200 two-color illustrations show you how to: make inlays . . . turn wood . . . rebuild panels . . . reupholster . . . reinforce joints . . . replace veneers . . . remove blemishes . . . imitate grains . . . ''antique'' surfaces . . . and much, much more!

Designing and Building Children's Furniture with 61 Projects—2nd Edition

A step-by-step guide to making all kinds of children's furniture and toys, from cribs, cradles, and desks, to a rocking horse, play house, and toy box.
Devoted entirely to children's furniture, this book shows you how to turn inexpensive materials into useful furnishings children will enjoy. You'll learn the basics of furniture making, along with some important woodworking tips and techniques. Packed with two-color illustrations and easy-to-follow instructions, this revised edition provides everything you need to construct useful, sturdy furniture that is as much fun to make as it is to use.

Designing and Building Outdoor Furniture, with 57 Projects—2nd Edition

Build beautiful, sturdy outdoor furniture and patio accessories.
This book is filled with practical, easy-to-understand instructions and detailed two-color illustrations. Even the novice woodworker will be able to make outdoor tables, chairs, benches, planters, and more. Advice is offered on tools, materials, and techniques. Fifty-seven projects are described in detail, from simple benches to a more complicated picnic table.

Designing and Building Colonial and Early American Furniture, with 47 Projects—2nd Edition

Capture the spirit and style of authentic Colonial and Early American craftsmanship
Build your own Shaker, Pennsylvania Dutch, and other Colonial and Early American style furniture for a fraction of what you'd pay for authentic antiques or even store-bought reproductions! Blandford provides expert guidance in such traditional woodworking techniques as joining, veneering, carving, turning, and molding. He also shows you how to recognize good furniture design, how to solve specific design problems, how to use power tools to save time without sacrificing design integrity, and much more.

No. 3074
$21.95

Designing and Building
Space-Saving
Furniture
with 28 Projects

2nd Edition

Percy W. Blandford

TAB BOOKS Inc.
Blue Ridge Summit, PA

SECOND EDITION
FIRST PRINTING

First edition copyright © 1976 by TAB BOOKS Inc.
Copyright © 1989 by TAB BOOKS Inc.
Printed in the United States of America

Library of Congress Cataloging in Publication Data

Blandford, Percy W.
    Designing and building space-saving furniture, with 28 projects /
by Percy Blandford. — 2nd ed.
        p. cm.
    Includes index.
    ISBN 0-8306-1274-2   ISBN 0-8306-9374-2 (pbk.)
    1. Built-in furniture. I. Title.
TT197.5.B8B527 1988
684.1'6—dc19   88-7784
                                           CIP

TAB BOOKS Inc. offers software for sale. For information
and a catalog, please contact TAB Software Department, Blue
Ridge Summit, PA 17294-0850.

Questions regarding the content of this book
should be addressed to:

    Reader Inquiry Branch
    TAB BOOKS Inc.
    Blue Ridge Summit, PA 17294-0214

Cover photograph courtesy of Armstrong World Industries.

Edited by Joanne M. Slike
Designed by Jaclyn B. Saunders
Illustrations by Grace Meyer

Contents

Introduction

B UILT-IN FURNITURE is a product of the age. It suits the modern way
of life. Besides its attractions in terms of space saving, capacity, and
utility, built-in furniture can be used to express individuality. In contrast,
quantity-produced freestanding furniture, which may be attractive both
in price and quality, is the same as other people have. Most of us have
to accept this, as the cost of craftsman-made furniture puts it beyond reach
except for the few with the necessary skill to make their own freestanding
furniture.

Although there are pieces of built-in furniture that can be bought as
quantity produced units, there are limits to what can be done along these
lines. Building in inherently means that the shape and size of the available
space has to be taken into account and the furniture made accordingly.
It is here that the home owner and amateur craftsman gets an opportunity
to exercise his or her skill in producing an individual item of furniture.
Fortunately, built-in furniture is generally simpler to make than
freestanding furniture, as the face is about all that is visible; the surrounding walls form a large part of the construction.

As nearly all built-in furniture has to be designed to suit a particular
situation, stock designs can only have limited value. Consequently this
book is more than a series of designs. What is of more use to anyone

looking for information on built-in furniture is information on tool handling, detailed construction work, and basic design considerations, and some suggestions of things to make that can be adapted to suit circumstances. That is what this book is all about, and I hope a great many readers will find enough information between these covers to move them to tackle more ambitious furniture projects than they previously thought they were capable of.

The Planning Stage

NOT SO VERY LONG AGO the amount of built-in furniture in many homes was small—possibly a few shelves in an alcove, or a small ready-made rack or storage unit hung on screws. In a modern home, built-in furniture is much more extensive, and in some rooms, there may be more fixed furniture than freestanding items.

TO BUILD IN, OR NOT TO BUILD IN

Of course, there are advantages and disadvantages of built-in furniture, but for most purposes, the advantages outweigh the disadvantages. Many considerations must be made—not all immediately obvious—and this chapter is concerned with first weighing the pros and cons, then generally planning built-in furniture arrangements. The rest of the book tells how to make it.

Advantages of Built-In Furniture

The term *built-in* can be applied to any furniture item that is fixed in place. Sometimes its attachment is only incidental, and the item is otherwise little different from a piece of freestanding furniture. This points to one reason for building in. If there is a risk of furniture being knocked over or moved out of position, there is a good case for fixing it to the wall or floor, or both. A tall glass-fronted display cabinet could be vulnerable if unattached, and the result of knocking it over could be breaking the crockery on display. That risk is completely removed by building in.

Besides giving rigidity and security to a piece of furniture, building it into a corner, an alcove, or merely against a straight wall usually simplifies its construction. The wall—and (often the floor and ceiling—becomes part of the structure. Only nominal framing may be needed on the contact surfaces wall, ceiling, etc.).

Choice woods are often difficult to get and very costly, but built-in furniture lends itself to the use of manufactured boards. It is possible to use ordinary particleboard or chipboard for internal parts, plywood or hardboard for parts against a wall or otherwise hidden. For faces, these materials can be bought already veneered or covered with Formica or similar plastic. These prepared boards can be very attractive, yet their use in some freestanding furniture would seem inappropriate.

Another good reason for built-in furniture is economy of space. In an alcove something built in will be the maximum size that can be accommodated, so its capacity will be as great as possible. A piece of freestanding furniture, even if specially made to go into place, will be smaller by a few inches all around.

Freestanding furniture, even if fairly close-fitting in a recess or corner, will collect dust around the neighboring surfaces, so periodically the furniture will have to be withdrawn for cleaning. Its built-in counterpart will have none of these dust traps. Meeting surfaces of close-fitting, freestanding furniture will be hidden most of the time. This means that parts made of choice wood will not be seen, so part of the article might be considered wasted. Of course, the table, cabinet, bookcase, or other thing can be removed at some later time and used elsewhere—something that cannot be done with built-in furniture. However, there is the possibility that the shaped parts will be a different color than those that have been exposed to light.

In general, most built-in furniture is easier to make than freestanding furniture. Some of the outline is already there as fixed surfaces of walls, floor, and ceiling. Parts can be prefabricated to fit or can be made and fitted in position. Usually parts of the structure are made up as units and fitted in place, then the next part is made.

Though poor craftsmanship is always to be deplored, one may make an internal part of a piece of built-in furniture to much less than perfection and it will not matter. Of course, the exposed surfaces must be as well made as in any other piece of furniture, but the need for highest-quality workmanship throughout is much less in built-in furniture.

Storage Space and Built-In Furniture. Most pieces of furniture are made to serve a need. They may also provide decoration, but their prime purpose is utilitarian. Things like chairs and tables are normally better if movable, although a fixed tabletop might sometimes be more convenient than a freestanding table. (There are examples of built-in desks, fold-down tables, and the like elsewhere in this book.) Seating can sometimes be built in—possibly around a window alcove—and the lower part can become storage space.

It is just this feature—storage space—that is often better provided by building in. Bookshelves are obvious examples. A greater capacity for books can be provided by simple shelves fixed to the wall than by any type of free bookcase. In a kitchen, worktops on built-in furniture that match the appliances can be much more convenient than a collection of freestanding items. They also make better use of the space in what is often not a very large room.

Even against a straight wall, fixed furniture takes up less floor space than comparable freestanding items. If the built-in article is arranged as a complex serving many purposes—storing books, providing a cocktail cabinet, housing a desk with stationery storage, and providing display space—it will take the place of several other pieces of furniture and thus free other floor and wall space. This may be even more of an advantage in a bedroom, where free floor space is sometimes minimal once the bed has been positioned. A combined unit with clothes closet, dressing table, and other services can be attractive and can take care of the occupant's needs in a way that would be difficult or impossible otherwise.

If you have recesses or alcoves in your home, building into them might be the only way of making good use of them. Otherwise they might become depositories for odds and ends in an untidy jumble. They may still be used for storage, but shelves, a top, and a door will bring order out of chaos and make these areas look much better.

Building in also has some effect on insulation and problems of heating or cooling. Built-in furniture gives extra thickness to the wall it adjoins, and this provides an extra barrier to heat or cold—particularly important along an outside wall. In some situations insulation material can be included in the back of the furniture to increase this effect.

Disadvantages of Built-In Furniture

Building in is, of course, more permanent than making freestanding furniture. A built-in piece becomes part of the house, unless you make it in a takedown form. If you own the house and intend to live there for a long time, this might be a good thing. If you expect to move in the near future, you should weigh the value of the furniture against the period of time you will be there and estimate how much it will add to the value of the house when you sell. If the house is not yours, you have to allow for the fact that you will have to leave the built-in furniture behind—without getting anything for it—if you move.

Even if the furniture is not a permanent fixture and you can dismantle it and take it with you, it will have been designed for a particular situation, and it may not be much use, without considerable alteration, in another home. This is particularly so with corner or alcove items in which corners are sometimes far from right angles. Furniture which goes against a flat wall is more adaptable.

PLANNING FOR BUILT-IN FURNITURE

You have to be satisfied that a particular piece of built-in furnitu' e is what you want, and in the right place and the right size, before you make and fit it. In most cases alterations are not easy, and producing something that proves to be unsuitable often means scrapping it and starting over. Early sketches are worthwhile, and it may be better to make a rough mockup of what is intended from card and scrap wood so that others concerned can see what is intended and agree to its construction. This might also reveal flaws in design. It could be that the proposed item would interfere with natural lighting, prevent a room door from opening, or do something else undesired. Such problems should be taken care of before you start the actual piece of furniture.

High Storage

A place where built-in furniture wins out over freestanding furniture is high in a room. Freestanding furniture is usually not very tall. A clothes closet might be high enough for the clothes to hang above one or two drawers and the top might still be far enough from the average ceiling to leave a space which could be useful, yet storage there results in an untidy pile. With built-in furniture the whole room height can be used.

A Basic Plan

Of course, ceiling-height storage might be too high for anyone standing on the floor to reach, but this is an opportunity to use space that is otherwise wasted to house things that are only infrequently needed. One possibility is bookshelves for reference books and others that are only needed occasionally (FIG. 1-1A). Another idea is cupboards with doors that hinge normally, slide, or swing up (FIG. 1-1B).

One of the attractions of making built-in furniture is that it is possible to make combined pieces that have several functions. An example is in a bedroom (FIG. 1-1C). In this case, just about everything is taken care of around the bed, but a room has four sides, and it is not good design to put everything to one side. In this case, the window is to the left side,

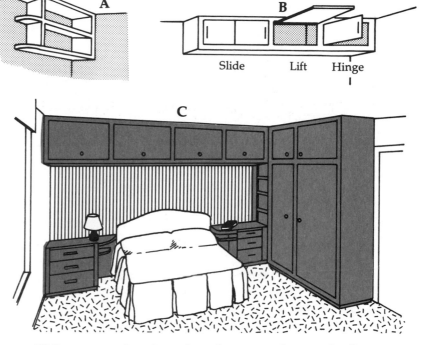

Fig. 1-1. Wall space out of arm's reach can be converted to occasional storage space for things seldom used, by building in bookshelves (A) or cupboards (B); one of these could be constructed above the doorway of the bedroom shown (C).

and a freestanding dressing table is the main feature of the wall facing the foot of the bed. A stool for the dressing table and a chair make up the furnishings.

This sort of thing does not design itself; there has to be some preliminary work, probably including several experimental layouts, before a pleasing result is achieved. If you are artistic you can simply sketch views as you hope they will appear, but you might find that, although your sketch looks good, the pieces won't fit in the available space. More design information is given later in the book as it relates to various items of furniture, but broadly the approach should be as follows.

A plan of the room can be drawn to any suitable scale. First draw and mark the location of any doors or windows. In the example, the walls at the head of the bed and by the door are involved (FIG. 1-2A). The bed and other things that will stand on the floor are also drawn to the same scale on card and cut out.

You will have to decide how wide you would like the bedside cabinets and how large the clothes closet will have to be for what you want to put in it. Sizes may have to be modified later, but move the pieces around

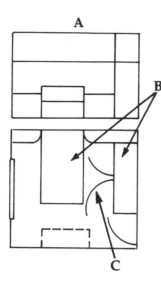

Fig. 1-2. The plan for a bedroom should include a drawing of the proposed placement of furniture against walls (A), cardboard furniture models that can be moved around on a floor plan for experimental positioning (B), and allowance for closet door swing (C).

on the floor plan to settle positions (FIG. 1-2B). Also consider the movement of doors. Will the clothes closet door clear the bed (FIG. 1-2C)? If not, the bed will have to be moved, and this affects the bedside cabinets, making one wider and the other narrower. If there just is no way for the closet door to swing, you will have to settle for sliding doors.

Also consider the room door. It if happens to be hinged on the side against the clothes closet, will it swing far enough? If not, the clothes closet might have to be moved, affecting the bedside cabinet, or it will have to be made narrower.

Having arranged the things on the floor to apparent satisfaction, how will they look against the walls? At the wall at the bed head, draw the bed, add the two cabinets, and allow space for the inset shelf that the clothes closet will determine. There could be a problem with the bedside cabinet that comes next to the clothes closet.

If drawers are involved, the near edge must be far enough out to clear the front of the clothes closet, and even then they can only be used when the closet door is closed. Will this suit your needs? If at some time you think there is a risk of someone pulling out a drawer against a partly open closet door and doing damage, would it be better to have a door on the cabinet, or merely shelves that could never lead to collision with the closet door?

At the other wall the closet can be drawn in and a block of shelves arranged over the end of the bedside cabinet. If there is a worthwhile space between the top of the door and the ceiling, it might be better to carry the upper part over the door (FIG. 1-3A). If you don't consider this worthwhile, the better plan might be to stop at the closet side (FIG. 1-3B).

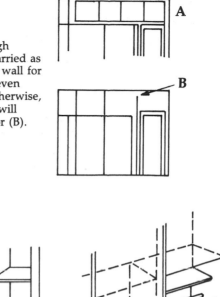

Fig. 1-3. If possible, high cupboards should be carried as far as possible across a wall for the best use of space, even over a doorway (A); otherwise, cupboard construction will have to stop at the door (B).

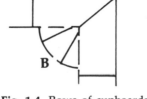

Fig. 1-4. Rows of cupboards that meet at a corner can overlap (A) or they can be separated by a mitered partition (B). No amount of space within built-in furniture should be left over; you can usually find a way to get to the extra space in a dresser (C) or closet (D).

The high storage space at the head of the bed will probably look best if it is at a matching height with the top compartments of the closet, as illustrated in the upper right hand portion of FIG. 1-1C. It does not have to be, but if the bottom edge is brought lower, what about the door near the corner fouling the closet door when that is opened? If both are hinged in the same corner, there is not much risk; but if the upper door swings the other way or upwards, it could strike the opened closet door. Sliding doors would avoid this, but sliding doors do not give as clear an access to the interior.

There is yet another problem, which is common to all built-in furniture that goes around a corner. What do you do where the two parts meet? At the top, one cupboard could be carried through (FIG. 1-4A), or there could be a mitered division (FIG. 1-4B). Also, if you don't want the lower part to be wasted space, you must provide access. If the bedside cabinet has a door or shelves, it could be carried through. If there are drawers, any access that way might only be possible by withdrawing the drawers, giving what almost amounts to a secret compartment, but that is not what is usually wanted. Instead there could be a lifting top over the corner, making this suitable for storage blankets and similar things, or it might be used for soiled linen (FIG. 1-4C). Another way would be to cut off the clothes closet wall so access is from inside the closet. The space might then be used for shoe storage (FIG. 1-4D).

Most aspects of planning the layout in this case have now been considered. After experimenting with your first drawings of the floor and two walls there might be many lines that you don't want that might confuse you when starting construction. At this stage I suggest that you trace over what is wanted and discard the original so there will be no risk of using the wrong drawing.

One final step in the planning stage is to arrange a simple mockup in the actual room. Position the bed where you intend it to be. If the floor is bare, mark where the other things are to come with chalk. If this cannot be done, lay down strips of wood to indicate outlines. Pivot other pieces of wood on nails to represent doors, and see that they have ample clearance. Use some scrap pieces of card, hardboard, or plywood as drawers and try pulling them in and out to see that nothing will come in their way.

Reasons for Planning

All of this might seem a lot of planning, but it is really just a logical reasoning involved. In most built-in furniture, except the simplest, the alteration of one part has to be matched by the alteration of another. It is obviously better to check all this and arrive at a satisfactory result before cutting wood and making joints. Once construction has begun, it is frustrating to realize that something has been overlooked and you will have to alter some wood and scrap other parts.

It can also be frustrating when making something like this bedroom furniture, in which many parts make up the whole, to find that somewhere along the line a measurement is wrong. It might only be a slight error where two parts that should be level are about ⅛ inches off, possibly not much more than the thickness of a pencil point against a rule. It could be a larger error perhaps, due to forgetting to allow for the *plinth*, or the thickness of a strip under a top, when measuring. This is human error that can happen to any of us, but you will reduce the risk by using a *rod*.

A rod is a strip of wood with key dimensions marked on it. In the example, it would be a strip of wood reaching from floor to ceiling.

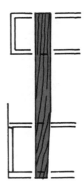

Fig. 1-5. It's always best to use a rod (wooden gauge) for marking out the placement of furniture parts. Errors are often made in reading rules.

Prominently marked on it are such things as the height of the plinth, the level of the cabinet tops, and the lower edge of the high units (FIG. 1-5). Measurements with rods and other devices are discussed more fully in the next chapter.

DESIGNS AND PREPARATIONS

With freestanding furniture there are plenty of designs available in magazines and books, with all sizes given and with step-by-step instructions and ample illustrations. With built-in furniture each item must usually be of an individual design, particularly if it is to fit into a recess or occupy a certain position on a wall. Although there may be instructions available based on how someone else did a job, these will almost certainly have to be modified to suit your needs. This means that anyone making built-in furniture needs to know a little about design so he or she can adapt a pattern that appeals and originate a suitable design.

Design Features

There are two main considerations in design: utility and appearance. There is no use making something pleasing to look at if it is unsuitable for its intended purpose. Similarly, it is displeasing to make something that fulfills its purpose but is ugly. Fortunately, fitness for purpose usually results in a pleasing design.

It is useful to consider the article to be made in relation to an average person. Assume a piece of furniture has working and storage areas. For standing, a reasonable work height is about 36 inches (FIG. 1-6A). For sitting, the work height is better at about 30 inches, with a seat level of about 17 inches.

Storage Items. For storage, the most convenient height for handling items, particularly if the items are heavy, is between waist and shoulder height, with a slight reach upward being preferable to much of a bend downward (FIG. 1-6B). Heavy-item storage levels should be between 36 and 72 inches or so (FIG. 1-6C).

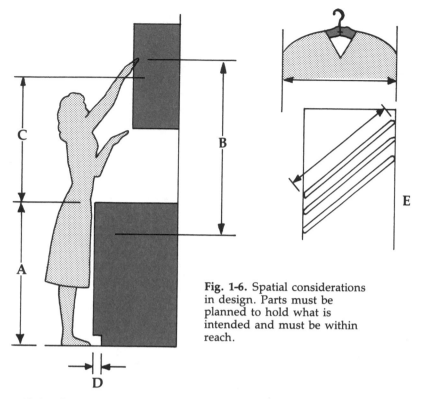

Fig. 1-6. Spatial considerations in design. Parts must be planned to hold what is intended and must be within reach.

If the furniture is not a working item like a kitchen cabinet or desk, it does not matter how the bottom is arranged; but if anyone is to stand facing the furniture, the bottom should be cut back (FIG. 1-6D) to give toe clearance and reduce damage from kicking.

If the furniture is for storage only, it will probably be made as deep as a recess will allow, or it will be extended from a wall as far as possible without interfering with the use of the room. If it is to be a working item, a back-to-front distance of not more than 24 inches is advisable, otherwise reaching to the back may be too much of an effort. If it is a clothes closet, about 22 inches should be allowed for the width of coats on hangers. If the width has to be less than this, the coats will have to hang diagonally (FIG. 1-6E), which reduces capacity.

Handles and Hinges. The positions of handles and pulls will have to be related to other design features, but if you want a full-depth door, the handle should be at the same height as room doors, or about 36 inches, so it can be reached without bending. For smaller doors a handle at exactly center height does not look as good as one above or below that—especially above. Drawer pulls look better and are more functional if placed above the center line (FIG. 1-7A).

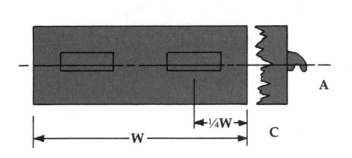
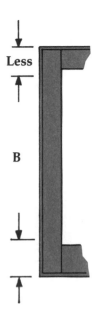

Fig. 1-7. The appearance of built-in cabinets and cupboards is always better if handles are above the center line (A), and hinge lower spaces are greater than higher ones (B). A rule of thumb for locating drawer pulls is to center them at one-quarter drawer width within the drawer edge (C).

Hinges on a door always look better if the space from the top is less than the space from the bottom (FIG. 1-7B). If both distances are the same, the lower distance looks less. How to space two drawer pulls cannot be settled geometrically, but one-quarter of the drawer width from each end is about right (FIG. 1-7C).

Shapes. Getting shapes that are pleasing depends to a certain extent on the designer's artistic ability, and this often comes with experience. However, there are a few pointers that can help. For most things the predominant lines should be horizontal and vertical. Diagonal lines are best avoided. There are occasions when diagonals can be introduced, but normally they should have a secondary effect.

Exact squares are best avoided. A rectangle is much better, particularly a length about 1½ times the width (FIG. 1-8A). If one rectangle comes inside another, it is better to keep the border fairly narrow (FIG. 1-8B). With the border exactly the same all around, the border at the bottom always looks narrower, so it is usual to make this wider (FIG. 1-8C). If you want something to appear tall or slim, include plenty of vertical lines (FIG. 1-8D). If you want it to appear broad or flat, use horizontal lines (FIG. 1-8E).

It seems more natural to use a heavier construction down low, so framing should be wider, where it is visible, near the bottom of a cabinet than higher up. In a two-part construction, such as a storage cupboard below and a display cabinet above, let widths of visible parts on the top part be narrower than those in the lower part.

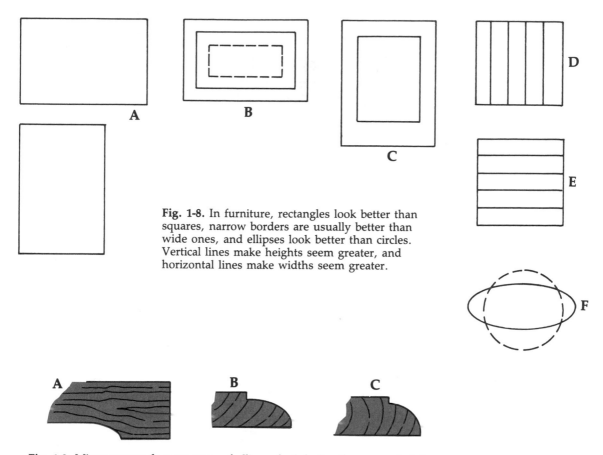

Fig. 1-8. In furniture, rectangles look better than squares, narrow borders are usually better than wide ones, and ellipses look better than circles. Vertical lines make heights seem greater, and horizontal lines make widths seem greater.

Fig. 1-9. Minor curves that are parts of ellipses look better than arcs of circles.

A similar idea applies to color. The "heavy" part should be at the bottom. If you are mixing woods or using different paints, make the lower part darker than the higher part.

In much modern furniture it is better to stick to straight lines, but if you want curves an ellipse will work better than a circle (FIG. 1-8F). Similarly, part of an ellipse is better than part of a circle for a cutout corner (FIG. 1-9A). Even with small things like the edge of a flap or table, an elliptical curve (FIG. 1-9B) looks better than a circular one (FIG. 1-9C).

Drawings. It is always helpful to make a drawing at the outset of a project. This does not have to be in great detail. Choose a convenient scale and get the main outlines down to the approximate proportions, at first in light lines. Then go over the lines representing the edges of framing, drawers, doors, and other prominent features so they show up clearly. You will soon see if the result is what you want and likely to look satisfactory.

If there are other nearby features in the room that will affect the final appearance, sketch them in to approximately scale. Stand back and look at the drawing propped up vertically. This is much better than viewing close to a drawing flat on a table.

Mating Surfaces

One thing that soon becomes apparent is that many homes lack precision in their construction. A home may be just as comfortable to live in with a corner at 85° instead of 90° and with a wall that has a slight curve and is not vertical, but problems appear when furniture has to be made to match.

Although the edges of furniture may have to be made to match any irregularities, it is important that paneling, doors, shelves, windows, and all the normally visible construction should be horizontal and vertical, rather than parallel to inaccruate surfaces. Any lack of squareness in these items will be very obvious.

Checking Levelness. A floor should be tested with a level (FIG. 1-10A). If the floor is very unlevel, it might be wiser to ignore it as a means of checking levels and use a false bottom as a base for measuring from, adding a plinth outside to disguise discrepancies (FIG. 1-10B). In some furniture it might be better to establish a horizontal surface at a higher level and use this as a reference for other surfaces. This could be a shelf or other salient level surface (FIG. 1-10C). With one horizontal surface established, other surfaces should be checked from it for levelness. The carpenter's level can provide a second check.

Many levels will also check vertical surfaces. If the level is not very long, use a straightedge that reaches somewhere near the height of the furniture for testing. There might be minor irregularities in a wall, and a short level might follow these and indicate a lack of trueness where the overall

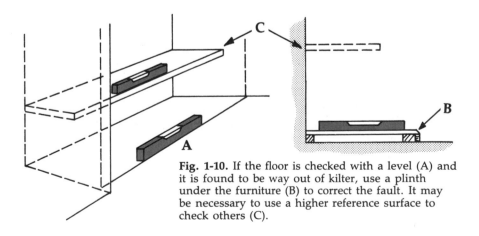

Fig. 1-10. If the floor is checked with a level (A) and it is found to be way out of kilter, use a plinth under the furniture (B) to correct the fault. It may be necessary to use a higher reference surface to check others (C).

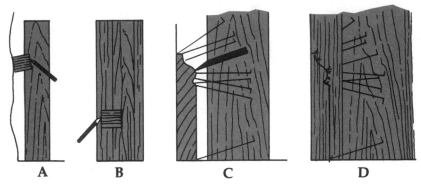

Fig. 1-11. Spiling techniques for fitting furniture alongside a wavy wall (A and B) or against an existing molding (C and D).

reading would be different. This is especially likely with plastered surfaces.

Spiling. Lack of verticalness at the back of a cabinet might not be of much consequence, but if the side of a recess has a variable line, the adjoining edge of the piece of furniture will have to be shaped to fit. This outline can be obtained by *spiling* (FIG. 1-11A). Hold a spiling piece—a strip of wood—vertically, then use a block of wood and a pencil to follow the line of the wall surface at the back of the cabinet. Then mark a scrap piece of wood as a template. Now put the spiling piece over it, put the block of wood against the pencil line. Use the pencil against the block to reproduce the line of the wall on the template (FIG. 1-11B).

Cut the template and try against the wall. If necessary the edge can be adjusted to suit, then you can use the template to mark the cabinet edge. Of course, the template step might be skipped and the cabinet marked directly from the spiling strip, but there is then a risk of losing verticalness of the other part of the cabinet wood if much adjusting has to be done to the edge.

It sometimes happens that you have to cut the fitted furniture around a base or picture molding. It might be simpler and better to cut this away so the furniture goes tight against the wall and the cut molding butts against it, but if there is any risk of damaging the wall in removing the molding, you should leave the molding in place. If the built-in furniture is to be removed at some later date, it is better to leave the wall and its molding undisturbed. In that case the molding shape can be obtained with a pointed spiling stick (FIG. 1-11C) and reproduced on the template by connecting marks around the point (FIG. 1-11C). There are adjustable templates that can be used, but these are limited to only a few inches.

Checking Angles. When furniture is to go into a recess, it is important to check the angles of the corners. If the furniture is made right-angled and the corner is wider than a right angle, there will be a gap at the front (FIG. 1-12A). If the angle is less than a right angle but the furniture is right-angled, it might go in and look satisfactory if it has been made to measurements at the front. If the measurements were taken at the back, however it will probably be too big to fit.

For anything of no great width, such as bookshelves, you can obtain the corner angle with an adjustable bevel (FIG. 1-12B) directly transferred to the shelf end (FIG. 1-12C). It is always bad practice to extend anything short to suit anything long, and there is too much risk of error to use this method for something much wider than the length of the bevel blade.

Convenient measurements can be taken in both directions from a corner, with one going at least as far as the furniture will reach. The distance

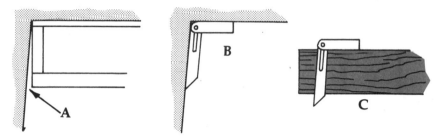

Fig. 1-12. A gap between the wall and the side of furniture in a corner can be avoided by first checking the corner angle with an adjustable bevel (B); the angle of the bevel can then be transferred to the furniture (C).

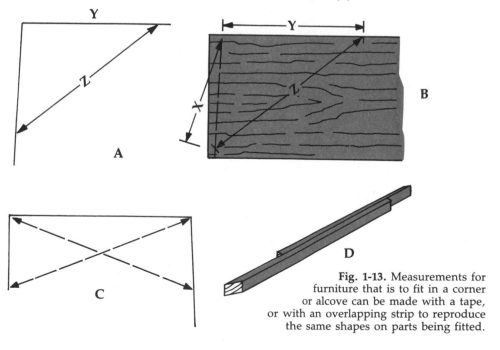

Fig. 1-13. Measurements for furniture that is to fit in a corner or alcove can be made with a tape, or with an overlapping strip to reproduce the same shapes on parts being fitted.

Z between these points is then taken (FIG. 1-13A). If the base measurement is taken along an edge, and an arc with the other wall measurement is swung with rule or tape measure from one point (FIG. 1-13B), a measurement of the diagonal Z will locate a mark through which a line (see dashed line) can be drawn at the same angle to the edge Y as the angle of the corner.

For a two-sided recess, take the measurements from opposite corners (FIG. 1-13C). Internal measurements may then be taken with an expanding tape rule, or two overlapping sticks can be used, with their overlaps marked so they can be put together again at the same distance (FIG. 1-13D).

For many assemblies, when there are errors in the walls, it is a good idea to use a piece of plywood as a template on which to base parts of the construction. The plywood can eventually be used for the top or some other part of the furniture.

2

Tools and Techniques

THE BEST METHOD OF MEASURING is to compare one part with another. If the piece can be placed against a part it is to match and marked from it, there is no need to bother about feet and inches.

MEASURING AND MARKING

Direct comparison reduces the risk of error to a minimum. This does not mean various measuring rules and tapes do not have a place—they are very important—but their purpose is to provide a means of comparison, and the woodworker, whether making new parts or repairing old ones, should look for ways of cutting out intermediate measuring steps.

Measuring

As we are in a world transition of measuring systems, any craftsman should be prepared to measure in feet and inches or in metric measure. This means that you should buy rules and tapes with markings in both systems.

It is, however, extremely unlikely that metric measure will completely replace the traditional measure for several generations. Even if there is a determined attempt to use metric measurements for new work, there will have to be reference to things that were made or built to the older system; and where they come in a round number of inches or feet, any conversion may result in unwieldly figures. For instance, the familiar 2-x-4-inch section is 51 x 102 mm. While new stock can be machined to 50 x 100 mm, combining the sizes in a structure could result in growing errors, or at least a slack fit. On things of larger size—such as an 8-x-4-foot plywood sheet, which converts to 2438 x 1219 mm—some modification of stock size will come to a round figure, but much existing design suits the older measurement. All of this means that woodworking craftsmen will have to be aware of possible differences and be prepared to adjust their measured work accordingly.

Linear Measurements. A folding rule is convenient for carrying. Most are quite thick, so if they are put flat on a surface, the graduations are high above the surface. This could result in errors of parallax (sighting). To avoid this, put the rule on its edges to bring the markings close to the surface (FIG. 2-1A). While a pencil dot might be all that is needed, it will be helpful in locating the marks later if they are *pecked* as shown in FIG. 2-1B. (The point of the V is the measurement point.)

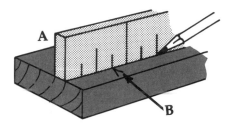

Fig. 2-1. Putting a rule (A) on edge (B) avoids errors of parallax.

The folding rule has practically been replaced by the tape rule, which stows compactly in its case and usually has a hooked end. This is the most frequently used measuring instrument in furniture work.

The folding and tape rules cannot be used for drawing straight lines and are not the most convenient tools for setting gauges or tool fences. Straight steel rules are better for these uses. Although a 12-inch rule is most common, a 24-inch or 60-mm one is better for bench work, both for accurate measuring and for drawing straight lines. Turned on edge it can also be sprung to curves that have to be drawn.

Most woodworkers use ordinary round pencils for marking wood. The point quickly blunts and frequent sharpening is necessary. The life of the point can be lengthened if it is sharpened to a chisel shape. Rub the point on a piece of fine glass paper glued to a strip of wood to maintain this shape.

The traditional carpenter's pencil has a rectangular-section lead in oval-section wood. This sharpens to a broad chisel point that has a long life. These pencils are worth buying if you can find them.

For greater accuracy, particularly where a cut is to be made across the grain, a knife can be used instead of a pencil. The traditional knife has an angled cutting edge across the end. A newer type has disposable blades and has other uses besides marking.

Dividers (FIG. 2-2A) can be thought of as only a means of scratching circles, but they are also valuable for comparing measurements and for stepping off distances. If rungs or rails have to be equally spaced, using dividers will ensure accuracy (FIG. 2-2B).

Calipers are really dividers with bent ends. The outside caliper (FIG. 2-2C) is used for checking across curves. A piece turned on a lathe cannot be measured across with a rule, but calipers can be adjusted to it and checked against a rule or the part the lathe-turned part is to fit. Inside calipers (FIG. 2-2D) serve the same purpose in hollows or holes.

Angular Measurements. The checking and measuring of angles—particularly right angles—occurs frequently in woodworking. The basic tool for marking and testing right angles is a *try square* (FIG. 2-3A). This can be all steel or have a brass-faced wooden stock and a steel blade. The

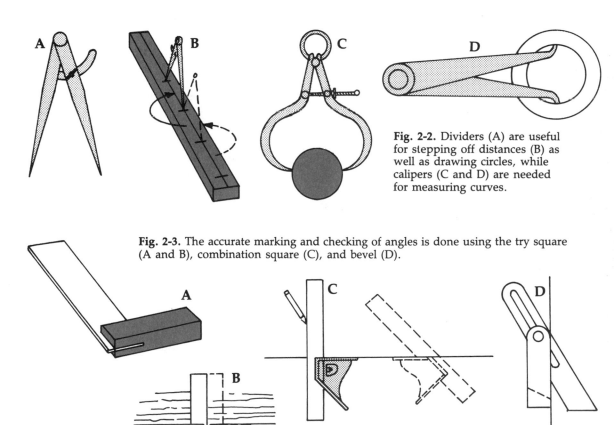

Fig. 2-2. Dividers (A) are useful for stepping off distances (B) as well as drawing circles, while calipers (C and D) are needed for measuring curves.

Fig. 2-3. The accurate marking and checking of angles is done using the try square (A and B), combination square (C), and bevel (D).

check for accuracy is to press it against a straight edge, draw a line along the blade, and then turn it over and see that the blade still matches (FIG. 2-3B).

Try squares are made in many sizes. For general work it is best to have one with a 12-inch blade. Instead of a smaller try square it might be better to have a *combination* square. The head can be locked anywhere on the blade so the blade length can be adjusted to suit what is needed. The other side will mark or test a miter of 45 degrees (FIG. 2-3C).

For angles other than 45 degrees or 90 degrees, an adjustable *bevel* is needed. This has a blade which slides in its stock and can be locked at any angle and extension (FIG. 2-3D). The bevel can be set to a protractor or an existing cut piece.

Marking

Lines parallel to an edge can be drawn by measuring two or more points and then laying a straight edge through them. In most cases, however, it is better to gauge the line. To do this, pull a notched piece of wood along with a pencil against its end (FIG. 2-4A). An experienced woodworker can make a reasonably accurate line with the pencil between first finger and thumb and the other fingers against the side of the wood, but this is not recommended.

A combination square is used in a similar way. With the blade set to the correct distance and a pencil held against the end, draw the square along the edge (FIG. 2-4B). A marking gauge uses the same basic principle with a scratching point. Wood and metal marking gauges can be used

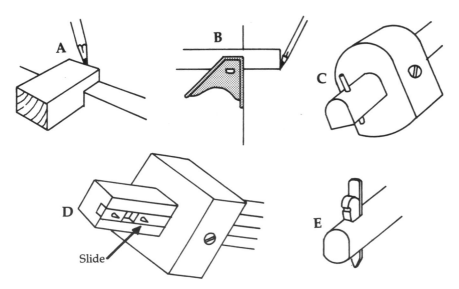

Fig. 2-4. Gauges can be used to mark lines parallel to an edge.

for distances up to about 6 inches from an edge. First, tilt the gauge (FIG. 2-4C) in the direction in which it is to be pushed. Curl your first finger over the top of the stock, then push your thumb behind the point, make sure all other fingers keep the stock pushed against the edge of the wood.

A *mortise gauge* is similar but it has two points that can be adjusted in relation to each other as well as in relation to the stock (FIG. 2-4D). It scratches two lines at the same time and gets its name from its use in marking out mortise and tenon joints, but it also has other uses.

If used for a mortise, a chisel is tried against the points so they are set to the correct width. The ordinary marking gauge scratches and might tear the grain. A cutting gauge has a knife blade, which makes a clean cut (FIG. 2-4E) and is particularly valuable for use across the grain. It will also cut parallel strips of veneer.

When almost all woodworking processes were done by hand, it was customary to prepare each piece of wood with a face side and face edge. These were the first side and edge, planed straight and at right angles to each other. They were identified by face marks (FIG. 2-5). Now that some processes are done more easily and more accurately by machine, there is not always quite as much need for face surfaces in all woodworking; but in furniture work a reasonable degree of precision is necessary, and it is wise to use these marks.

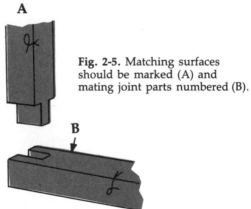

A

B

Fig. 2-5. Matching surfaces should be marked (A) and mating joint parts numbered (B).

When a framework is being made, all marking is done from the face surfaces, with try square, marking gauge, and other tools used there— not the other way. Then when the piece is assembled, all face marks are kept one way (usually outside). This results in correct matching on the face side, and any errors due to difference in thicknesses all come on the other side.

Coupled with this is the need to identify joints. Even when joints are cut mechanically, it is unlikely that all joints in a particular assembly could be interchangeable. This means that joints should be lettered or numbered. These marks are usually made so they come together then a part is unlikely to be reversed.

It is possible to have all surfaces apparently flat and all corners right angles but the work out of true. This is called *in winding*. An example is in a long board that is flat, as tested crosswise at several places, but twisted. The amount of twist can be more easily seen if a pair of winding strips are used. These are two matching strips of wood, thick enough to stand edgewise. One might have pieces of contrasting color insets at its ends to aid sighting. If these strips are placed at opposite ends of the board and sighted along, any twist can be seen (FIG. 2-6).

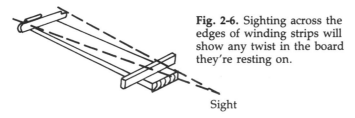

Fig. 2-6. Sighting across the edges of winding strips will show any twist in the board they're resting on.

Sight

Another twisting problem might occur during assembly. Much furniture construction consists of frames built up and then joined to each other to make a boxlike framework. If any part of this assembly is out of true, it becomes very apparent to any observer. For this reason, opposite sides should be made up first. When one side is assembled, its corners should be checked with a try square, then by measuring diagonals (FIG. 2-7A). The second assembly should be made facedown on top of it to match.

Both assemblies have to be checked for twist by sighting across them. Usually it is best to leave them under clamps or weights on a flat surface for the glue to set (FIG. 2-7B). If the box is longer one way, accuracy is usually more easily obtained if the long sides are assembled first.

When fitting the other parts, check for squareness in the short sides and measure diagonals as well. It is then necessary to check for twisting

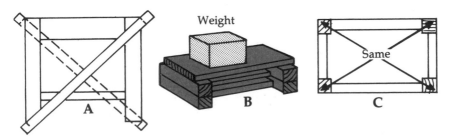

Fig. 2-7. Comparing the diagonal dimensions of a rectangular subassembly provides extra assurance of its geometric accuracy. Subassemblies being glued for a boxlike structure should be held under weights (B) to avoid warps; check a trail assembly for trueness (C) before final gluing.

or winding across the assembly in both directions. If you can stand the assembly on a known flat surface, it can be held down under weights. Before doing this and before the glue sets, check squareness from above (FIG. 2-7C), and probably from the bottom as well on many assemblies.

Finally, stand back as far as you can and look at the assembly from several directions. You do not have to be very experienced to notice lack of squareness anywhere, and it is better for you to see it now and correct it than to leave it for a visitor to point out later.

HOLDING DEVICES

For most woodworking processes both hands are needed for things other than holding the wood, so the wood must be supported and held in a way that suits the operation. Although a limited amount of work can be done with improvised equipment, and there are sometimes occasions when it is necessary to make do with something that is not up to the desired standard, good craftsmanship is dependent to a very great extent on the way the wood being processed is held.

Bench Work

The first requirement is a bench. The important part is a stout, wide board for the front edge. This is usually of hardwood and is upwards of 2 inches thick to withstand hitting without noticeable bending. It can be supported by a front apron almost as thick (FIG. 2-8). The legs must be sturdy, and if the bench is freestanding, it should be of sufficient size to resist turning over or moving. The bench can be built onto a wall so that maximum rigidity is obtained.

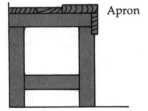

Fig. 2-8. The heart of a woodworking shop is a rigid bench topped with thick hardwood that is supported by an apron.

Apron

If a bench is unavailable, a stout board with a vise can be clamped to a table, but this is much less satisfactory.

A bench should be at a comfortable height for working, and for the average person, this is about 30 inches. It is best to make it as long as the available space will permit. The greater the length, the easier it is to accommodate long pieces of wood and plane or otherwise work them accurately.

Besides the bench you will probably need trestles, or sawhorses, preferably two of the same height. These are best at a height convenient for sawing, which means about 18 inches. They need not be very well made, but they should be rigid. Old chairs without their backs can be used, but it is better to make horses with the legs splayed wide to resist tipping (FIG. 2-9).

Fig. 2-9. Probably the most convenient height for a sawhorse is 18 inches. It need not be made neatly, but its legs should take a wide stance; a pair of sawhorses can support doors and other large pieces being planed.

For right-handed working, it is best to mount a vise towards the left end of the bench. A large professional-type vise with wood over the jaws is best (FIG. 2-10A). A quick-release action is handy, but not essential. Smaller clamp-on vises have their uses, particularly when work has to be done away from the shop, but good work is much easier with a substantial vise.

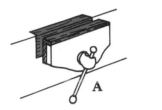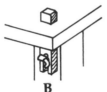

Fig. 2-10. The bench vise (A) and bench stop (B) are fixed devices used to hold and steady work.

There should also be a bench stop. For planing and some other processes, the wood needs something to prevent it from sliding off the bench. Simplest is a strip of wood nailed across the bench end, but it is better to have something that can be adjusted out of the way. There are metal stops that recess into the top of the bench and can be adjusted up and down with a screw action. The objection to these is that they are metal; if a plane hits one, its blade is damaged. Many workers prefer a wooden stop because of this. A simple one is tightly fitted in a hole through the bench and can be forced up and down. An improvement is a screw and nut that lock the stop in position (FIG. 2-10B).

Another essential piece of bench equipment is a bench hook, or preferably a matching pair (FIG. 2-11A). The hook is made to go over the bench as far as the edge of the front board, and the cross pieces are held with glued dowels rather than screws, so there is no metal for saw or other tools to touch.

The most common use of the bench hook is to press wood against it with one hand while sawing with the other. So that the saw does not

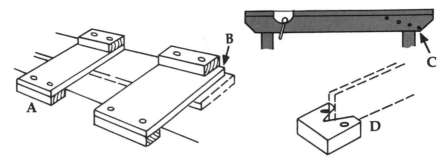

Fig. 2-11. One of the pair of bench books shown (A) has a recessed top piece (B) that allows a saw to strike its base rather than the bench. Dowels inserted into one of several holes in the bench (C) can give a vise a helping hand in holding work; the V-block (D) is another temporary wood-holding aid held by dowels.

drop through and damage the bench, one end can be cut back (FIG. 2-11B). If the wood being worked is long, the second hook provides additional support. It is best to regard the bench hook as disposable. Chopping with a chisel and other cutting can be done on it rather than damaging the bench top. The hook can be scrapped and replaced when it gets badly damaged.

When long pieces of wood are held in the vise, it is helpful to have holes to take pegs at the other end of the bench in order to provide additional support (FIG. 2-11C). If you want to plane thin wood on edge, it can be done more accurately if the wood is supported on the bench. A V block (FIG. 2-11D) will steady the wood. If you include two dowels to fit holes in the bench top, the bench top can be removed when it is not needed.

Traditional hand-working cabinetmakers used a *shooting* (planing) *board* to hold wood to be planed on edge. Machine planing has superseded this method for production planing, but anyone making or repairing furniture should know about it. A long-soled plane is used on its side, and the wood is supported at about the height of the center of the blade. A shooting board may be 3 feet or more long and arranged with a block to hold in the vise (FIG. 2-12A). A smaller one could be made like a bench hook and used with a low-angle plane for squaring across the end grain.

If corners have to be taken off a square section, as when chamfering for decoration or preparing wood to turn in a lathe, a trough is valuable. Two pieces are beveled at about 45 degrees and fastened together, then a stop is recessed into them. A trough wider than it is deep (FIG. 2-12B) can rest on the bench top. It may have extension pieces for use when working with extra-long wood. If the rough is deeper than it is wide (FIG. 2-12C) it can be held in the vise.

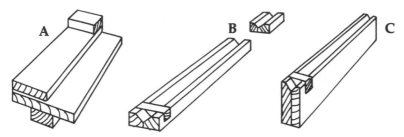

Fig. 2-12. Planing aids.

Clamping

You will need clamps in as wide a range as possible. The basic C-clamp (FIG. 2-13A) is used in many sizes for holding parts together while joining them or for holding wood while it is being worked on.

A variation on the C-clamp has a sliding head (FIG. 2-13B). This increases the range, but usually the reach is not as great as in a C-clamp equal to its greatest capacity, so pressure cannot be applied as far from an edge. Wooden clamps with pairs of screws (FIG. 2-13C) have their uses, but they cannot exert as much pressure.

A *bench holdfast* is a type of clamp you are likely to use frequently. In its simplest form the stem goes through a hole in the bench top; then tightening the screw causes this to hold by leverage and friction. A better type has serrations in the stem to engage with matching projections in a metal collar recessed into the bench (FIG. 2-14A).

For clamping outside the range of C-clamps, there are *bar clamps* (FIG. 2-14B) sometimes called *sash* clamps from their original use in clamping sash windows during their making. Usually a pair of bar clamps are

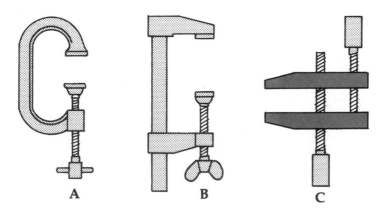

Fig. 2-13. A variation of the C-clamp (A) has a sliding bead (B); a near kin to these is the wooden clamp (C).

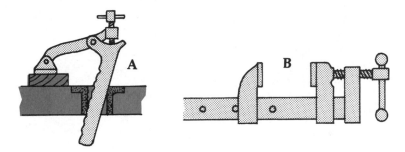

Fig. 2-14. The bench holdfast is aptly named: Its serrated stem grips a grooved collar imbedded in the bench. For work of a size beyond the capacity of a C-clamp, there is the bar clamp (B).

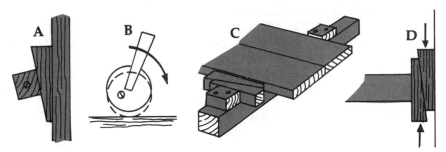

Fig. 2-15. Pieces being glued can be pressed together with a wedge action.

needed. Although a straightforward squeeze is all that is needed, a distorted assembly can be pulled true by setting a bar clamp slightly askew. There are heads similar to those on bar clamps available for fixing to the edge of a board, usually with pegs through holes, but these are not usually as effective as an all-metal bar clamp.

There are many improvisations that can be used for holding and clamping; most are based on a wedge action. A wedge pressing against a block can provide a considerable pressure (FIG. 2-15A). This is useful for holding laminations around a former. A similar action comes from a cam. A disk is given a lever and mounted on a screw through an off center hole (FIG. 2-15B). This acts as a rotating wedge.

A single wedge does not give a parallel action, so it may move parts being clamped. The remedy is to use a pair of "folding" wedges (FIG. 2-15C). If they are driven against each other, the pressure is tremendous and parallel. This method can be used to make an effective bar clamp (FIG. 2-15D). The idea can be used on an assembly: a block of wood can be temporarily screwed to a part so a pair of wedges can work against it to provide pressure on another part.

Rope and cord are used for clamping, sometimes with wedges. Rope knotted as tightly as possible around an assembly can have one or more

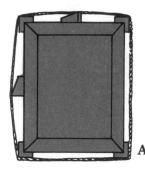
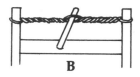

Fig. 2-16. Rope can be tightened around parts being glued with wedges (A) or a Spanish windlass (B).

wedges driven beneath it to exert more pressure. For a frame or other structure, the rope should be padded so as not to pull into the edges of the wood; shaped wood blocks are best (FIG. 2-16A).

Another way of tightening a rope is to use a *Spanish windlass* (FIG. 2-16B). It can pull parts of a chair back together or put pressure on parts that have to be forced into a curve. Since there is considerable strain on the cord, it is usual to have many turns with the ends tied. A lever, often a hammer handle, is put in the turns and twisted. When pressure is sufficient the end of the lever can be lodged against a part of the structure or tied alongside the twisted cord.

SAWS AND SAWING

Sharp saws are essential to good work. The best sharpening or setting is done professionally by machine, although it is possible for the craftsman to maintain his own saws. In either case, it is obviously best to have saws that keep their edges as long as possible. This is related mainly to the quality of the steel and the way it is tempered, and these things in turn are usually related to price, so it is always advisable to buy the best saws you can afford.

Much wood, particularly those varieties used for furniture, is bought already cut to section, and the craftsman making furniture is mostly concerned with saws that will cut wood to length and make joints. He is less concerned with the saws used to convert wood from the log or reduce the sizes of bulk lumber.

Saw Teeth

Two general forms of saw teeth are used—those for cutting across the grain and those for cutting along the grain. To provide clearance, nearly all saw teeth are set by being bent alternately each way so the *kerf* or cut, made in the wood is wider than the thickness of the steel plate from which the saw blade is made (FIG. 2-17A). Saws used on green wood (freshly felled and containing much sap) have considerable set, for a wide kerf;

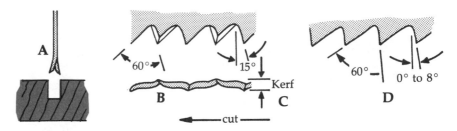

Fig. 2-17. When a saw blade cuts, it makes a kerf wider than itself (A). The teeth for cutting across the grain (B and C) differ from those used with the grain (D).

but even the fine saw used for small pieces of wood that are correctly seasoned must have some set unless the cut is merely superficial.

Teeth for cutting across the grain must sever fibers with a knife action. Teeth for cutting along the grain cut with more of a chisel action. *Crosscutting* teeth can be used along the grain, although not as efficiently; they are commonly used for all directions when cutting joints.

Similar tooth shapes are used for handsaws and power saws, although power saws can be given gullets (channels) between groups of teeth to clear sawdust, and there are tooth shapes used on some power saws to give special characteristics. Many of these could not be applied to handsaws, as an electric motor has a reserve of power denied to the human muscles.

Saw teeth for cutting across the grain have an included angle of 60 degrees (FIG. 2-17B), which allows for sharpening with a triangular file. The sharpening angle gives alternate teeth knifelike edges on opposite sides of the blade. Up to half the depth of each tooth is bent outward to give the width of the kerf (FIG. 2-17C).

The coarseness of saw teeth is defined as the number of points in an inch. The usual range of handsaws have teeth between 5 and 18 points per inch, although fine piercing saws can have many more, and large saws for cutting up trees may have fewer. Power saws tend to have coarser teeth than handsaws used for the same purpose.

Saw teeth for cutting along the grain also have an included angle of 60 degrees; but the forward edge is nearer upright, and the teeth are filed straight across (FIG. 2-17D). Setting is similar to crosscut teeth, but often coarser because there is more of a tendency for the wood to bind on the sides of the saw.

Handsaws

The general-purpose handsaw for cutting on the bench is a *backsaw* (sometimes called a *tenon* saw) about 12 inches long and with 14 or 16 teeth per inch. The back is stiffened with a piece of steel or brass, and

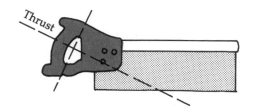

Fig. 2-18. A properly designed backsaw applies thrust directed toward the middle of the cutting edge.

the handle may be wood or plastic. There are variations in handle forms, but the important thing is a comfortable one-hand grip with a thrust directed to somewhere near the middle of the cutting edge (FIG. 2-18).

The best control is obtained with one finger held straight. Most saws have their own slight perculiarities. A craftsman gets to know his own favorite saw and instinctively gives any necessary little bias to achieve an accurate cut.

For finer work there may be a smaller backsaw, sometimes called a *dovetail* saw, only 8 or 10 inches long, with 18 points per inch.

Panel Saw. Backsaws are mostly used for nearly horizontal cuts on wood held in the vise or on the bench hook. Usually the cuts are not of very great extent, although thin sheets of plywood may be conveniently cut for long distances with a backsaw. For cutting thicker wood or for other heavier and longer cuts, the proper tool is an ordinary *handsaw* or *panel* saw.

Much of this sort of work can be done more easily with small power saws, but a craftsman needs one panel saw for work the power saw cannot manage. A saw with a blade about 24 inches long and crosscut teeth, about eight per inch, should do.

A saw of similar general appearance but with teeth for cutting along the grain is called a *ripsaw*. Whether one is needed or not depends on the type of work, but if hardwoods have to be cut by hand along the grain, this is much easier to use than a crosscut saw.

Although a panel saw may be used on the bench and can be made to cut down wood held in the vise, the usual method is to lay the wood on one or a pair of horses, to kneel over the wood, and saw downward at an angle. The angle of cut depends on the wood. If it is comparatively thin, it will cut more cleanly at a flatter angle, as more teeth will be in contact at one time; but if it is thick wood, the effort needed for each stroke is reduced if the saw is more upright, so that a shorter length of wood surface is presented to the saw at each stroke.

A point to watch in any sawing is that the method of support does not encourage the kerf to close on the saw as the cut progresses. It is better to saw wood supported at one side of the cut than between two supports. The free part should be held so it does not drop, and the last few strokes should be taken lightly so the grain fibers do not break out.

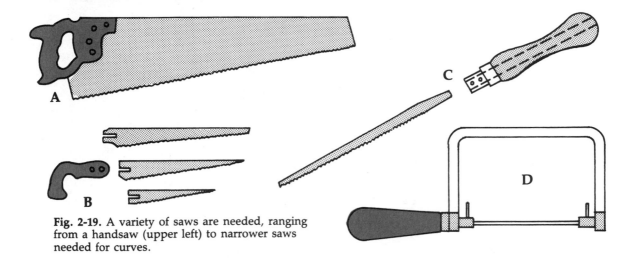

Fig. 2-19. A variety of saws are needed, ranging from a handsaw (upper left) to narrower saws needed for curves.

Handsaws for Curves. Ordinary saws can only make straight cuts or follow a very slightly curved line. Special handsaws for cutting curves have been largely replaced by power saws, but there are sometimes places where the power saw cannot reach or where the intricate shapes are better cut by hand.

FIGURE 2-19A and B contrasts the panel saw (A) with the curve-cutting handsaws. The type at B has a thicker blade to compensate for narrow width from teeth to back. These are sometimes called *compass* saws and may be supplied with one handle and a set of three or more blades of different widths for curves of different sizes. A very narrow saw of this type, which usually fits through a pad handle, is called a *keyhole* saw (FIG. 2-19C).

For anything finer than this, the blade has to be tensioned. A *scroll* or *coping* saw (FIG. 2-19D) has a sprung frame. The even finer *fretsaw* usually has a rather deeper frame. In both cases the blades are disposable, and several spares should be kept.

When using any saw on a curve, it is important to keep it cutting when altering its direction, or it may twist and break in the cut.

Power Saws

The power saw for straight cuts is a table saw with a circular blade. There are general-purpose blades, but if a great variety of work is to be tackled, you will have to use several blades. One with crosscut teeth like those of a handsaw will make finer cuts and leave surfaces that need less finishing than a saw with larger combination teeth.

A large saw is generally more useful than a small one. Of course, it should have ample power, as there is often a tendency to make such a saw do work really outside its capacity. Also, as teeth get blunt the load

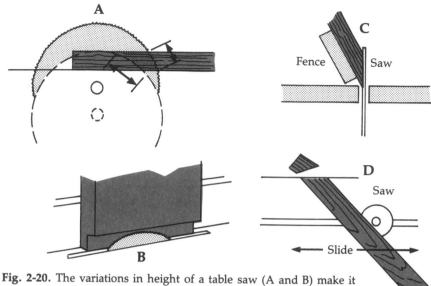

Fig. 2-20. The variations in height of a table saw (A and B) make it versatile. Adjustable fences permit the accurate cutting of angles (C and D).

on the motor increases considerably. Either the saw spindle should have a rise-and-fall adjustment, or the table should have a similar adjustment.

For ordinary cutting, the maximum amount of blade should project. This puts less load on the motor than if the blade has less projection, because not so much saw edge is in contact with the wood at one time (FIG. 2-20A). Considerable overload can occur if the wood is not fed straight, so the fence or other guide should be kept truly parallel with the saw.

Much of the joint cutting that can be done by hand may also be done with a table saw by adjusting the depth of cut and fence distance (FIG. 2-20B). Angles may be cut with a suitable sliding guide (FIG. 2-20C) or adjustable fence (FIG. 2-20D) with a precision greater than that obtainable with a handsaw.

The alternative to pushing the wood against a rotating saw is to have the saw move in relation to the wood. Such a saw may be completely portable, within the limits of its power cable (FIG. 2-21A), or it may be mounted to give a limited range of movements in a *radial arm* saw (FIG. 2-21B). While both saws have many uses, some of these are more applicable to carpentry than furniture making. A table saw is a better first choice.

Some modern furniture has fairly severe straight lines, but other modern furniture and most colonial and antique furniture includes plenty of curves. Anyone making reproduction pieces or repairing old furniture needs to be able to saw curves with reasonable accuracy, if subsequent

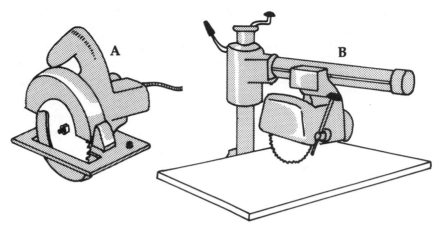

Fig. 2-21. A portable power saw (A) is an alternative to a handsaw; a radial arm saw (B) differs from many other power saws in that it moves in relation to the wood.

work with other tools is to be kept to a minimum. There are machine tools that make accurate sawing easier than with comparable hand tools.

Band saw. A *band saw* has a continuous flexible cutting band over two or three wheels. The depth of throat limits how far a cut can be made from an edge (FIG. 2-22), but even a small band saw can be made to cut curves in quite thick wood, providing progress is kept slow.

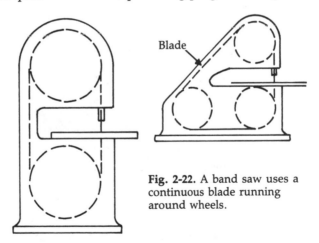

Fig. 2-22. A band saw uses a continuous blade running around wheels.

Blades are easily changed. A narrow blade is used to follow a tight curve. The strength of a wider blade can be used for bigger curves. A band saw can also be used for straight cuts. Although it does not have the ability to keep on its straight course without much guidance, it is convenient for short cuts.

Saber Saw. Another power tool for curves is the *saber saw*, which is moved in relation to the wood to be cut. The saber saw works with a reciprocating motion and cuts on the upward stroke. This means that any raggedness from the cut is on the top surface. (With a band saw it comes below.) The actual movement of the saw is not great, so although the blade might pass through wood 2 inches thick, it would not cut it very well, if at all. A saber saw is more suited to thinner wood. It does not have the band saw's limit of distance from an edge.

As saber saw blades are unsupported at one end, they have to be thick for stiffness. Different sizes and types of teeth are available. Coarse teeth are needed for thick and soft wood, but a better surface is obtained on hardwood with fine teeth that can still cut the particular curve. There are saber saw blades to suit metals and plastics, as well.

Other Power Saws. An alternative saber saw is one in which the same type of blade points upwards through a table and the wood is moved against it. The cut is then downward, so the better surface from the cut is on top and it is easier to follow a line. Except that a saber saw is not restricted in the distance of the cut from an edge, a band saw is generally preferable, as cutting is more accurate and the cut edge is better.

There are also power scroll saws or fretsaws, which will take the same blades as the hand frames. They are less popular than they once were, but anyone wishing to make the intricate pierced chair backs or other fretted work of some furniture styles will find these tools best.

SHAPING AND SMOOTHING

Anyone working on furniture needs a variety of chisels. These are end-cutting tools, and their effectiveness depends on their sharpness.

Types of Chisels

Common chisels come in widths from ¼ inch, upwards. The widest commonly needed is 1½ inch. The general-purpose type often described as a *firmer* chisel, has a flat, parallel-sided blade (FIG. 2-23A).

Most new chisels have plastic handles that can be hit with a hammer or mallet, but traditional chisels had wooden handles and were hit with wooden mallets. Firmer chisels can be bought with a beveled edge (FIG. 2-23B) that penetrate wood more easily and can get into corners. Longer and thinner versions are *paring* chisels, which are not intended to be hit.

A chisel curved in cross section is a *gouge*, and these come in similar widths. A gouge sharpened on the inside (FIG. 2-23C) is used for paring internal curves, and one sharpened outside (FIG. 2-23D) is used for hollowing. At one time, very stout mortise chisels were used for chopping out joints, but it is more usual now to remove the bulk of the waste with a drill and do final shaping with firmer chisels.

A large range of gouges in many widths and degrees of curvature are used for carving. There are a few carving chisels and tools of special form,

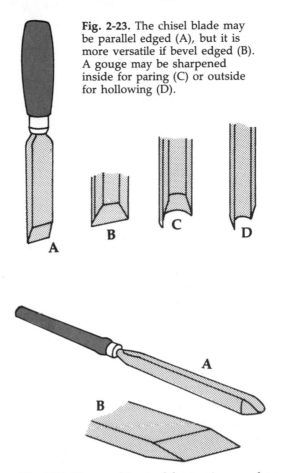

Fig. 2-23. The chisel blade may be parallel edged (A), but it is more versatile if bevel edged (B). A gouge may be sharpened inside for paring (C) or outside for hollowing (D).

Fig. 2-24. The roughing tool for turning wood on a lathe is a long gouge (A), the finishing tool is a chisel sharpened on both sides (B).

but most tools in a carver's kit are gouges. A wood turner uses chisels and gouges, but these are longer and stronger than those used for other woodworking, and the handles are long to provide leverage. The gouge blade can be square across or rounded. It is thick and is sharpened on the outside (FIG. 2-24A). Turning chisels are sharpened on both sides and usually have skew ends (FIG. 2-24B).

Planes

Planes may be regarded as devices to control the cut of a chisel. A chisel may cut freehand to almost any thickness of shaving, but the plane restricts the cut to the removal of a comparatively thin shaving. Traditional wooden planes are just about obsolete, but if one becomes available, it is probably worth acquiring. The modern steel plane has lever and screw

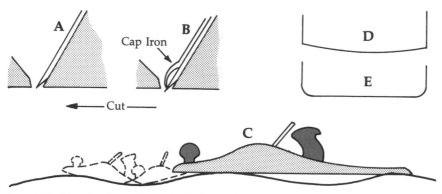

Fig. 2-25. Simple planes have single irons, but most modern planes have a cap iron to break off shavings (A and B). To true an uneven surface, there is an advantage in a long plane (C). A plane's cutting edge may be rounded for rough and quick cuts (D) or straight with rounded corners for finishing (E).

adjustments, as well as a sole that stays true (unlike a wooden plane, which had to be trued with another plane occasionally).

A plane can have a single *iron*, or blade (FIG. 2-25A), but most planes intended to produce a smooth surface also have a *cap iron* (FIG. 2-25B). (The word *iron* is still used despite the fact that parts are now being made of steel.) The cap iron breaks off the shaving into segments, and this discourages tearing up the surface of the wood.

Length of sole is an advantage when uneven wood has to be trued. A short *smoothing* plane might follow undulations, but a long plane bridges the hollows and takes off the high spots first (FIG. 2-25C).

A *jack* plane (the name comes from *jack-of-all-trades*) is used to get rough or sawn wood approximately to shape. The mouth of the plane is set fairly wide (there is usually a screw adjustment), and the blade is sharpened to a slight curve (FIG. 2-25D). The cap iron is set ⅟16 of an inch or more back from the cutting edge. The plane can be set to take off fairly thick shavings, but might not then leave a good surface.

The long *trying* plane is used next if there is need for truing in the length, and a smoothing plane removes roughness. In both cases the plane is set to only take off a fine shaving. The mouth is set narrow, and the cap iron is fairly close to the cutting edge, which is sharpened straight across, with the corners rounded.

A plane should be used, if you are right-handed, with the left hand on the knob and the right hand on the handle. The wood should be on the bench against the stop or in the vise so it is possible to stand against the side of the bench near the end of the wood and push the plane away from you. This gives the best control and achieves best results. Standing at the side of the work causes excessive strain on the muscles, and plane control is less precise.

A *block* plane is a one-handed tool about 7 inches long with a single iron set at a low angle. The better block planes have adjustable mouths. They are mostly used for cuts across the grain, but they are useful for any fine cut, such as taking the sharpness off an edge.

There are special planes for cutting rabbets and other grooves. An ordinary plane cannot go close into a recess, but, if the iron runs the full width, it can. There have been *rabbet* planes of ordinary appearance except for the cutting edge going full width, but most such planes are narrower.

When given a fence to control depth and width of cut, the tool may be called a *fillister*. A plane for making a groove is called a *plow*. It has a narrow sole and a kit of blades of various widths, plus depth and side fences. Modern fillisters and plows are all metal, and there are combination planes that will do these and other jobs. However, power tools can perform similar functions and might be preferable.

At one time, any cabinetmaker had a large collection of *molding* planes, each with its bottom and blade shaped to the profile of a molding. Modern furniture has less molding, and what there is either bought ready-made and stuck on instead of being part of the base wood, or it is produced by a spindle molder or other mechanical means. Old molding planes are still valuable in reproducing or restoring old furniture.

A simple plane for getting to the bottom of a groove, as in a dado joint, is little more than a chisel through a block of wood (FIG. 2-26A). This is an *old-woman's-tooth*, or router. A metal version has a bent blade with more of a cut than a scrape.

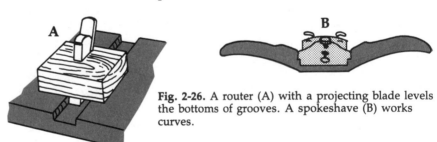

Fig. 2-26. A router (A) with a projecting blade levels the bottoms of grooves. A spokeshave (B) works curves.

Most planes are used on flat surfaces only, although a plane with a flat sole can be used on an externally curved surface. There are planes known as *hollows* and *rounds* that are shaped to work straight edges of matching curved sections. Planes have been made with adjustable curved bottoms to work lengthwise hollows.

For curves in the length there are *spokeshaves* (FIG. 2-26B). These have handles at the sides and a little cutter that can have adjustments like a plane. There might also be a flat bottom for working external curved edges, or a rounded bottom for planing hollows. Today much of the work of spokeshaves is better done with a *Surform* tool, which may be flat or curved and is used like a file. Its cutter is a replaceable blade with a series of rasplike cutters that let the shaving pass through.

Planing Machines

Planing machines have their uses in the home shop, but quite often their capacity is insufficient for all work undertaken. A planing machine has revolving cutters. The depth of cut is controlled by regulating the difference in height of the feed and takeoff tables. The size of the machine is the width of maximum cut.

A planing machine can also be used at its edge for cutting rabbets. Some planing machines can be moved over the wood surface in the same way as a hand plane. Both types of machine certainly reduce labor. Manual planing hard and cross-grained wood can be very tiring.

Using the Planing Machine. Machine planing, by its nature, produces a series of curved indentations. If the wood is fed very slowly over the cutters, these will not be very obvious; but they would show through a finishing treatment if no other work were done on the surface.

Although machine planing is often followed by sanding, it is better in good-quality work to remove all signs of machine planing by using a smoothing plane before sanding or other work. If the cutters of a planing machine are not in perfect condition, they might pound the surface as well as cut it, later causing unevenness or uneven absorption of stain or polish. Hand planing removes this risk.

Molders and Routers. Rotating cutters, power-driven at very high speeds, have taken over from molding planes and other tools that worked recesses, rabbets, and patterns. As with most other power tools, there are static and portable versions. In the static version the motor is below a table, and the cutter projects above it in a space in an adjustable fence. Wood passed along the fence is cut with the reverse of the profile of the rotating cutter. This *spindle molder* can have plane cutters to make rabbets, or shaped ones to produce moldings.

The portable tool is called a *router*. The motor is on top and is fitted with handles. The cutter projects through a broad base, which is cut away to expose the cutter. There are depth adjustments, and various guides and stops can be used. The tool can also be used to level the bottom of a groove or to make the groove without any need for sawing or chiseling first. A plain ½-inch cutter, for instance, can be led across a piece of wood, and the result will be a groove of even depth with clean sides. A guide can be used for straight or shaped cut, or the cutter can be guided around a marked line.

Tool Sharpening

Chisels and plane irons must be frequently sharpened if they are to work efficiently. Sharpening is done in two stages: (1) grinding, which is the removal of the bulk of the unwanted steel, and (2) honing, or whetting, which is the actual production of the cutting edge. Sharpening can be done many times with most tools before grinding becomes necessary again. With some tools, such as the thin irons in some planes, you may never need to resort to grinding. However, if there is much thickness of steel, grinding saves time and effort at the sharpening stage.

Some craftsmen have their tools ground professionally from time to time, but in most shops it is convenient to have a grinder. At one time this was a large sandstone wheel, turned slowly by foot or hand and kept moistened by dripping water. Modern grinding is usually done with a smaller, fast-turning grinding wheel which is used dry. The moistened sandstone wheel had the advantage of not drawing the temper of the steel.

When steel tools are made they are first hardened; then the degree of hardness is reduced enough to suit the purpose of the tool. If the tool is later heated so that colored oxides appear on the surface, further softening takes place. The amount of softening is indicated approximately by the area of colored oxidation. Although the oxides are easily rubbed off, the tool is only restored to condition by grinding past the area that was softened. When grinding on a high-speed dry stone, be sure to have a container of water nearby and dip the tool in this frequently.

Grinding. A chisel and the thicker plane irons are given two distinct bevels (FIG. 2-27A). The sharpening bevel starts quite narrow, then further sharpening widens it. After many sharpenings an unduly wide bevel is produced and the tool must be ground again. If the grinding is done on a small wheel, the tool may be against the rest and the wheel circumference. It should be moved from side to side, particularly if the wheel is narrower than the tool edge. This minimizes overheating and grinds the edge evenly.

If the tool is held continually at the same angle, the final bevel will be hollow (FIG. 2-27B). Slight hollowness might not matter, but it could re-

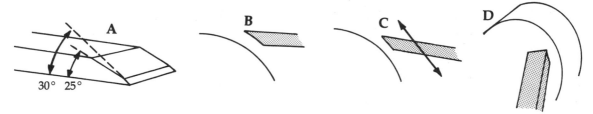

Fig. 2-27. On many woodworking tools there is a main grinding bevel and a shorter sharpening bevel (A). Grinding is done on a revolving stone (B through D).

sult in weakness that might lead to either breaking or vibration in use; so it is better to move the tool up and down slightly during grinding to give a flatter bevel (FIG. 2-27C). If grinding can be done on the flat side of the grindstone, this ensures flatness (FIG. 2-27D), although there is more risk of grinding unevenly.

Honing. Final sharpening is done on an oilstone. There are natural stones (such as Arkansas) and manufactured stones (such as carborundum). Usually the natural stones are finer than the manufactured ones, although it is possible to get double-sided manufactured stones with fine and coarse grits. A useful size for dealing with most tools is about $8 \times 2 \times 1$ inch. It is advisable to mount the stone in a wooden block. The oil used on the stone should be thin—sewing-machine oil rather than automotive oil.

Sharpening of chisels and plane irons for normal purposes should be done on one side only. There are guides which clamp to the tool and roll along, holding it at the correct angle. If you want to sharpen the tool freehand, hold it with one hand and apply pressure with the other. The important thing is to maintain the same angle for the length of the stone. There might be a tendency to dip the hands at the far end of the stroke. Besides rubbing up and down the stone, move the tool about to keep wear on the surface even (refer to FIG. 2-28). Angles are only approximate.

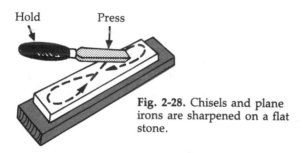

Fig. 2-28. Chisels and plane irons are sharpened on a flat stone.

The need for sharpening can be seen sometimes as a line of reflected light when examining the blunt edge. Continue rubbing on the stone until this disappears. Wipe oil off the tool and examine the edge. When the side being sharpened has been rubbed down to nothing, a sliver of steel will be rubbed off. This is quite minute, but when viewed across the blade, it is a sure sign that sharpening has been achieved. You can feel the difference by sliding your finger gently down the flat side towards the edge. Remove this *wire edge* by rubbing flat on the stone a few times. To make sure it's gone, slice the edge across a piece of scrap wood.

For the best edge sharpen the tool completely on a coarse stone, then repeat the process on a fine stone. If you were to examine the sharpened edge under a microscope, it will reproduce the size of the grit in the stone in a sawlike edge. The coarser the grit, the faster it cuts; so sharpening on a coarse stone gets a reasonable edge quickly. But if you follow with a fine stone to rub away all the marks of the coarse grit, the result is a better cutting edge.

Knives are sharpened in a similar way, except both sides should be rubbed on the stone. Carving gouges are often given a slight bevel inside. Turning chisels are sharpened on both sides, as a knife is.

The outsides of gouges can be sharpened on a flat oilstone by rolling the tool as it is rubbed. Insides have to be dealt with by an oilstone having a curved edge, or *slip*. There are several forms of these slips, usually with several sizes of curves on the same piece of stone. Usually the slip stone is rubbed inside the gouge like a file. An inside-sharpened gouge cannot be ground on a normal stone, so all of the sharpening inside is done with a slip, and the wire edge is rubbed off the outside with a flat stone. If it is the outside that is sharpened, the slip is only needed to remove the wire edge by rubbing lightly inside.

Scraping And Sanding

Sometimes the grain is such that you cannot achieve a smooth surface by planing. The old-time cabinetmaker scraped with a piece of broken glass, but a better tool is a steel cabinet scraper. This is a piece of saw steel. The edge is filed true, and both sides of this are turned over by rubbing very firmly either with a hard round steel rod or the flat of a chisel (FIG. 2-29A). The scraper is pushed to a slight curve and moved over the wood at an angle that makes the turned-over edge scrape a very thin shaving off the wood (FIG. 2-29B).

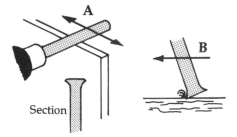

Fig. 2-29. By turning over the edge of a piece of steel (A), a scraper (B) can be formed.

You can also use handled scrapers that can be pulled over a surface for a similar effect; some have throwaway blades that ensure a good cutting edge without the sometimes awkward setting of the burr of the edge of a cabinet scraper. As wood with awkward grain is often used on furniture because of its attractiveness, scraping might be the only way of bringing the surface to an acceptable condition.

Sanding. Sanding should only be regarded as a final process before staining and polishing. Too often a power sander is used for processes that should have been done with a cutting tool. Sanding does not always remove wood. Fibers may be turned over instead of being rubbed off by excessive sanding. Sanding is an important final process, but the other steps should be done properly first.

The word *sanding* is a carryover from the days when abrasive paper was coated with sand. It is now coated with powdered glass, garnet, and many other types of manufactured abrasive grits. The backing may be paper or cloth. Older adhesives were not immune to dampness or sometimes to heat, so they would give up and the grit would be wasted. Modern abrasive cloths and papers have very tough adhesives, so the grits have longer lives.

Hand sanding is done with paper used loose in the hand or wrapped around a block. A piece of scrap wood is suitable, but cork and rubber sanding blocks that give a little resilience, which is preferable. Although power sanding may be used, finish with a final hand sanding if you want the best possible finish.

A power *orbital* sander takes flat sanding paper similar to that used for hand sanding (FIG. 2-30A). It is clipped to a backing pad, and the motor, which may be an electric drill, gives it a very rapid vibration over a small orbit. This can take the place of hand sanding for finishing, but it cannot be expected to sand away much wood.

A *disk* sander has a hard rubber disk mounted in an electric drill chuck which holds a circle of abrasive paper (FIG. 2-30B). Such a tool is not of much use for finishing a surface, as it leaves a series of curved scratches. It is more useful at places like multiple joints, where pieces come from

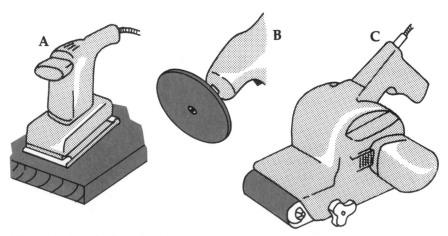

Fig. 2-30. An orbital sander (A) gives the smoothest results, but a sanding disk (B) will more quickly remove wood. A belt sander (C) also works quickly, without making the unwanted curved scratches a disk does.

several directions and have to be leveled. It can also be used on rounded parts, particularly where there is end grain.

The power tool for in-line sanding is a *belt* sander. The abrasive cloth is in the form of a wide belt that passes around rollers and over a pressure pad (FIG. 2-30C). In one form the tool has handles and is moved over the wood like a plane. Alternatively the sander may be static and the wood moved over it.

A mishandled orbital sander is unlikely to do any damage, but it is all too easy for disk and belt sanders to mar a surface if used in unskilled hands. They are all right for coarse sanding, but finishing is often better completed by hand.

Power sanding can produce a lot of dust. Belt sanders usually have extractors to take away most of the dust; but if much power sanding is done, there should be good ventilation, and you should always wear a mask.

MAKING HOLES

The portable electric drill is now the primary means of making holes, and it is often the first power tool in a tool kit. However, there are occasions when other means of making holes are preferable.

Brace

The traditional tool for making holes in wood is a carpenter's brace (FIG. 2-31A). One of these incorporating a ratchet should be in the kit of anyone expecting to do much furniture repair or construction. Bits fit in the brace with a square-tapered shank (FIG. 2-31B). This gives a positive, nonslip drive, which is sometimes difficult to obtain when a large-diameter bit on a round shaft is fitted to the self-centering chuck of an electric drill.

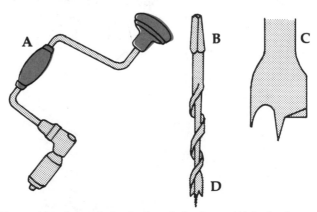

Fig. 2-31. For making larger holes by hand, the brace (A) is the best tool. For deep holes the bit should be parallel (B), but for shallow holes the spade bit (C) is simpler. A screw point pulls the bit into the wood and reduces the need for heavy pressure on the brace (D).

Bits

The simplest center bits (FIG. 2-31C) make clean holes in thin material. If holes are to go deeper, they can be kept true by a twist bit. There are several forms, but the Irwin bit (FIG. 2-31D) is one example. The screw point pulls the bit in, and your energy is only needed to turn the brace.

Another use of the brace is as a screwdriver. A screwdriver bit in the chuck stands the best chance of moving a stubborn screw, either in or out. There is no other way of obtaining so much torque while maintaining enough pressure to hold the tool in place.

A brace is also the best tool for countersinking. A power drill, even a multispeed one on its slowest speed, really turns too fast for proper countersinking. This is even more true when countersinking metal. If a hinge needs the screws set in deeper, the slow turning of the brace gives better control, and the countersink bit actually cuts better.

For large holes an expanding brace-bit is likely to produce a better and cleaner hole than any of the devices used in power drills. Such a bit has an adjustable cutting edge that can be set to cut different diameters. The bit is usually supplied with two adjustable pieces to cut up to about a 3-inch diameter.

Electric Drills

A difficulty you might have sometimes with an electric drill is restraining it. If you have to drill a small hole only a short distance to take the point of a screw, it is easy to go too deep or wobble the drill and make the hole too big. In this case, it is probably better to use a small wheel brace, which is much easier to control (FIG. 2-32A).

However, for small holes use a *bradawl* (FIG. 2-32B)—a tool so simple that it is sharpened to a chisel edge. To operate, enter across the grain and giving half turns in each direction while pushing in. It does not remove wood. Because of this a screw is likely to have a better grip than if the usual drill had been used to remove wood.

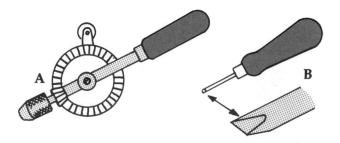

Fig. 2-32. Small holes can be made with metalworking drills in a wheel brace (A) holes for small screws may be made with a bradawl (B).

For woodwork, particularly if you want to use wood-boring bits of diameter larger than the chuck capacity, your electric drill should be adjustable for slow speeds. Then cuts will be easier to control and hole edges made cleaner. When holes go right through, take the drill into scrap wood on the far side, or preferably stop when the point shows through, then drill back from the other side.

Metalworking drills up to about ¼ inch are satisfactory for holes in wood, although they tear the fibers and do not leave clean edges. For sizes larger than this there are adaptations of the same form of drill with spurs and a center point (FIG. 2-33A). They will make straight, clean holes to their full length.

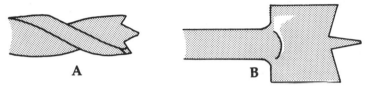

Fig. 2-33. For power drilling, bits can have relatively simple points.

Above this size there are spade bits (FIG. 2-33B), with a form that would be unsuccessful in the slow-turning carpenter's brace. But at higher speeds they make good holes, although they may wander if taken too deep.

For much larger holes there are hole saws and other devices that use cutters like sections of hacksaw blade or cutters that can be moved in or out, but these may not be as satisfactory as an expanding bit in a brace.

For much woodwork the electric drill is used freehand. However, accuracy depends on the eye. This also applies to using a brace. The operator can see the direction the drill is going from one way, but it is worthwhile having someone else viewing from about a right angle to the operator's view as well.

For accurate centering, make a dent for the start of the drill, even if the location is shown by two crossing pencil lines. A pointed awl can be used, or a center punch similar to that used for marking metal for drilling but with the point ground finer (about 30 degrees).

Where greater precision is needed, as when drilling dowel holes that have to be square to the surface, it is a help to have the electric drill in a stand, preferably a heavy one rather than the light one sometimes offered for amateur use. This is also suitable for use with attachments for drilling a series of holes to remove the waste in a mortise accurately. With the stop usually provided on the column of the stand, it is possible to control the depth of drilling precisely, which is important in such jobs as getting a series of turned posts set in equally or avoiding screw holes going too far and breaking through the other side.

Making Holes   45

Deep And Large Holes

If holes have to be taken very deep—as when putting an electric wire through a lamp standard—there is often a difficulty in keeping any drilling device straight, because wood is a natural material, and wanderings and variations of hardness in the grain may deflect the bit.

It is sometimes possible to make the piece in two parts or cut the wood to be used down the center. The hole is then made by grooving the two halves and gluing them together. With the strength of glues available today, the properly assembled parts should be at least as strong as the solid wood.

Long holes can be started with normal drills, with great care to obtain straightness, preferably using the electric drill in a stand for greatest precision. If the hole is to go through, it can be started from both ends. The tool for going deeper is an *auger*. This is a long twist bit, with a socket for a handle at the end instead of a shank to fit a brace (FIG. 2-34). With the first hole as a guide, this should work its way through without straying.

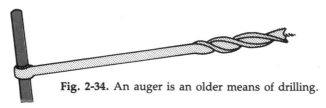

Fig. 2-34. An auger is an older means of drilling.

Withdraw the auger occasionally to clear waste. Otherwise the work can build up, and in wood of thin section, it could exert enough pressure to cause the wood to burst. In some woods it may be a help to reduce friction if you grease the twisted part with candle fat, but do not use ordinary oil.

There are special augers supplied for use in some lathes for turning long standards that have to be bored. A long auger to be used in a brace can be made by welding an extension on an ordinary woodworking twist bit.

When holes larger than those that can be made with any expanding bit are needed, it is possible to saw them, but it is very difficult to get a true circle with a clean edge. A power router may have an arrangement for allowing it to travel in a circular path, possibly by using a spike or nail through a hole in its adjustable fence. This can be used to make a true circle with a clean edge. Of course, it is limited in depth. Most cutters will cut through about ½ inch.

If the wood is thicker, go as deep as the cutter will go, then remove the rest of the waste with a jigsaw or other saw and carefully work the edge of the circle with gouges or a Surform tool.

3

Fastenings

IN THE BEST FURNITURE CONSTRUCTION, most joints are fitted and glued and have no metal fastenings. Where metal fastenings are needed, these are screws rather than nails, except in places that will not be seen. In less important furniture there might be more use of screws, nails, and other metal fastenings.

Many modern glues have such strong adhesion that they can be relied on even in places where they do not have the benefit of cut joints to relieve the glue of some of the direct load. With some glues the joint might be stronger than the wood, so wood fibers give way before the glue line in a test to destruction.

GLUES

Until World War II the common woodworking glue was made from bones, hooves, and other animal products. There were liquid glues in cans and tubes, but most glue was heated for use. It had adequate strength, as shown by the many old pieces of furniture still in sound condition; but this type of glue weakened to the point of becoming useless in damp conditions and would also soften if it became hot.

Animal glue is obsolescent, but it might be needed to match existing glue in restoration work. It is not compatible with modern glues, so any remaining in a failed joint should be scraped away before using another glue.

Another glue that dates from before World War II and is still in use is casein (*Casco* is one trade name). This is derived from milk. It is usually supplied as a white powder to mix with water into a paste. It has reasonable strength and some resistance to dampness, but immersion will soften it (although strength might return when it dries out). Casein still has uses for large laminations and other constructional woodwork inside buildings, but for furniture construction the craftsman in the home shop will find other glues more useful.

Synthetic Resins

Most woodworking glues are synthetic resins. As they are often known only by trade names, it is not always easy to identify them. Careful reading of the description or instructions will give you a clue to the type. If an adhesive is described as being suitable for fabric, paper, and other things besides wood, it is unlikely to have the maximum strength needed for joints in furniture construction, although it may be quite satisfactory for light decorative work or toys. If the glue is in two parts, that is a sign that it is a strong, waterproof one. If it is a one-part glue and the information on the container only mentions wood, it is also likely to be a good glue for furniture joints, although it might not be a good choice for anything that will be exposed to rain.

One of the powerful synthetic resin glues is resorcinol. Its glue line is a reddish-brown color, which makes it undesirable on some woods. It is used in plywood and some commercial production, but it can only be used on a close-fitting joint and must be clamped tightly. It does not bond to the resins used with fiberglass, so it might be unsuitable for furniture that combines wood and fiberglass. Although it may have some uses in the home shop, there are other glues more generally useful.

A good, general-purpose, two-part synthetic resin is based on urea. It is not so fully waterproof that it will withstand very prolonged immersion, but otherwise, once it has set, it will retain a strength at least as great as the wood in any conditions furniture is likely to meet.

In one form the glue is a syrup with a shelf life of a few months. Alternatively, it may be a long-life powder to mix with water to make the syrup. With this there is a catalyst (hardener), which is a mild acid. When catalyst and syrup are brought together, a chemical reaction drives out the water and the glue sets permanently. The process cannot be reversed. The catalyst may be mixed with the syrup before use; then the mixture must be used in the time specified by the maker (20 minutes is typical). Alternatively the syrup may go on one surface and the catalyst on the other so that reaction does not start until they are brought together.

In another form both catalyst and glue are in powder form and may be together in one container. So long as the powder mixture is dry, the glue has a long storage life; but when water is added, reaction commences and the glue has to be used in the time indicated on the container.

Urea glue is best used on a reasonably close joint, but this is not as crucial as with resorcinol. Great pressure is not needed—clamping need only be enough to maintain a close contact. Setting time varies according to the catalyst and temperature. In most cases the joint can be handled and worked within a few hours, but strength continues to build up, probably over several days or weeks. Urea glue may be used with wood and fiberglass.

There are glues with bases other than urea. If in two parts, they are probably at least as strong as urea. The glue with the greatest strength and versatility is epoxy-based,, but it is expensive and so is not usually chosen when another glue will do. It is a two-part glue that not only joins wood to wood but will join almost any material, including metal, to the same or some other material. Most synthetic glues have to be used above certain minimum temperatures (normal room or shop temperature is satisfactory), but epoxy can be used close to freezing.

Using Glue

Some woods will discolor if the glue parts are mixed in a metal container or applied with a metal-bound brush. Mixing in a throwaway plastic container and applying with a piece of wood will work better. Mix glue and catalyst by hand. A power mixer might introduce too many air bubbles. Also, if any joint is too open or there is a part to be built up, sawdust can be mixed with the glue until it has the consistency of putty. This can then be pressed or molded to shape and will have a strength comparable to the plain glue.

If plain glue is used in bulk, it will craze as it sets and will have no strength. With sawdust the glue bonds the tiny particles of wood, and will not craze. Using this mixture instead of Plastic Wood or other filler provides strength, but a filler would only provide shape.

SCREWS

Wood screws are described by: their length from the surface of the wood, their thickness by gauge number, the type of head, and the material from which each is made. There is no easier way of familiarizing oneself with screw sizes than by examining a selection, since the gauge numbers do not represent sizes easily visualized. Except in the smaller sizes, the even-number gauges are more easily obtained than the odd-number ones. Some generally useful sizes are ½ × 4 inches, ¾ × 6 inches, 1 × 8 inches, and 1½ × 10 inches; but all lengths may be thicker or thinner.

Unless there is a need for something else, flathead screws are commonly used (FIG. 3-1A). Roundhead screws (FIG. 3-1B) are not usually used directly with wood, but they are suitable for some metal fittings. The oval head (FIG. 3-1C) also looks well where the screw head is visible on a fitting. If a panel has to be removed occasionally, ovalhead screws through cup washers (FIG. 3-1D) are a good choice.

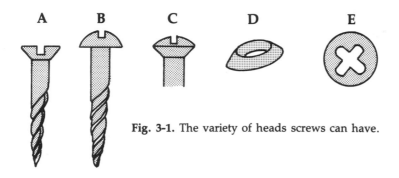

Fig. 3-1. The variety of heads screws can have.

General-purpose screws have straight slots, but Phillips and other comparable screws have star-shaped recesses (FIG. 3-1E). These are intended to prevent slippage with power screwdrivers in production work, but there are also hand screwdrivers to fit.

Most screws are bright steel. There is a risk of rusting, not only from dampness in the air but from chemicals in some wood; so for the best cabinetwork, use brass screws, which are less likely to corrode. A rusted steel screw in some oak might seize so it cannot be withdrawn, and it will eventually corrode to the breaking point.

Stainless steel, bronze, and other metals, and some plastics, are used for screws for special purposes, and most metal screws can be obtained plated to match the finish of the fittings they pass through.

Except for the smallest screws in softer woods, it is important to drill first. A screw usually has to pull two pieces together by squeezing the upper part between the screw head and the lower part gripped by the thread. Consequently there should be a clearance hole through the top piece (FIG. 3-2A). If the plain shank of the screw will continue into the lower piece, the clearance hole should go that far as well. There is no fixed size of lower hole for each screw, as the type of wood affects it. A small screw that does not have to go far in a softwood might cut its own way in, or a bradawl hole might be sufficient.

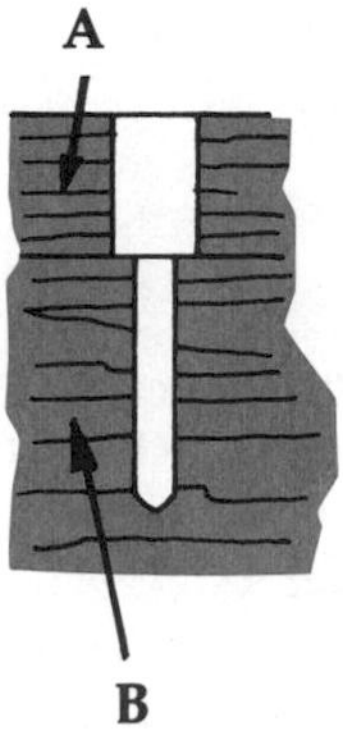

Fig. 3-2. Holes should be drilled to clear the screw shank (A) and be the tapping size for the threaded part (B).

In harder woods make the hole about the same as the core diameter of the thread. The screw can be left to cut its own way for perhaps two threads (FIG. 3-2B) in many woods, or the hole might have to go the full depth in really hard woods.

A flathead will pull in flush in softwoods and some plywood. Hardwoods will require use of a countersink bit, but even then there will be slight pull-in, so be careful not to countersink too much.

Screwdrivers should have ends which make a reasonably close fit in the screw head. This means having several screwdrivers. A long screwdriver is easier to use than a short one, but in furniture construction there are often places where a long screwdriver will not go. A collection of plain screwdrivers is worth having.

Additionally there may be ratchet and pump-action (Yankee) types with various points. A pump-action screwdriver may also take small bits for making the screw holes.

Sometimes the screw heads must be hidden. In this case the screws can be counterbored to put the heads below the surface. Drill a hole larger than the screw head, and plug after the screw has been tightened (FIG. 3-3). For the best effect, cut the plug cross-grained from a piece of wood that matches that being fastened. This can be made with a plug cutter, which is like a hollow bit used in an electric drill stand.

Fig. 3-3. A screw head can be sunk below the surface of a piece of furniture and concealed with a plug.

Keep the ends of screwdrivers filed or ground so they do not have rounded corners or edges. A worn screwdriver or one of the wrong size can jump off the screw and mar the adjoining wood.

NAILS AND TOOLS FOR NAILING

Nails are classified by their length. Although they are made to gauge thicknesses, there is usually little choice, and the thickness usual for a particular length will have to do. There is a system of *penny* sizes for nails—for example, 2d. is 1 inch long, 60d. is 6 inches long; however, it is probably better to avoid this system and order nails by length.

There is a very large range of nails available, mostly for purposes other than furniture making. Common box nails have flat heads (FIG. 3-4A). These are usually bright steel. The head gives a safe grip, particularly for a piece of thin plywood at the back of a cabinet or similar construction. There are different sizes of heads, but none is likely to be acceptable on a finished, exposed surface.

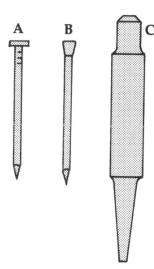

Fig. 3-4. Box nails (A) can't be easily concealed, but a casing nail (B) can be driven below the surface with a punch (C) and covered with stopping.

Nails may be bronzed or otherwise treated to improve their appearance. There are brass, copper, aluminum, and other metal nails, but some of them are inclined to bend or buckle if holes are not drilled.

Some nails are obtainable with ringed shanks. The rings give the nail something of the grip of a screw, but if it must be withdrawn, it will tear up the surrounding surface.

If nails are to be used in a place where the surface is visible, use nails with only slight heads. Larger ones are *casing* nails and finer ones are *finishing* nails (FIG. 3-4B). These can be driven below the surface with a nail punch (FIG. 3-4C), then the head can be covered with stopping.

In good furniture, nailing should be kept to a minimum, but sometimes molding or a decorative piece has to be fixed in this way. The strips holding glass in a cabinet door may also be nailed. If furniture is to be fixed to a masonry wall and nails are used instead of screws in plugs, there are hardened-steel masonry nails which can be used. Screws are preferable to nails for most furniture construction.

Nails in general carpentry are usually driven without any predrilling, but in the hardwoods and sometimes in narrow sections used for furniture, it is often advisable to drill for nails, particularly if the nail is to come near an edge. The hole in the upper piece may be just slightly undersize, while the one in the lower part may be about half the nail diameter and not taken the full depth. Much depends on the wood.

If a nail bends when being driven, it is usually wiser to withdraw it and use another than to straighten it and continue. Pincers or a claw hammer will remove the nail, but be careful that surrounding wood is not damaged in the process. Put a piece of thin wood where the pincers will lever.

The spacing of nails or screws is a matter of experience. When covering a framework with plywood, spacing around the edges should be closer than fastenings driven into intermediate frames, and at the edges it might be best to have a few closer fastenings near the corners. Nails driven alternately at opposite angles (FIG. 3-5A) in dovetail fashion will have an increased grip.

Almost any hammer will drive nails, but if one is bought for furniture work, it is useful to have a cross peen (FIG. 3-5B), which will go between finger and thumb when holding a small nail or hit in a recess that will not admit the flat peen. Nails in awkward places are best driven with the aid of a punch. For the pinlike nails often used in cabinetwork, a very light hammer (about 4 oz.) is best.

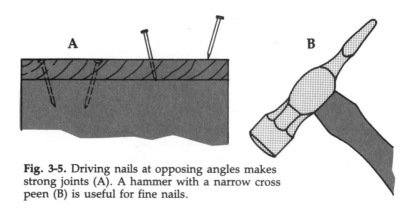

Fig. 3-5. Driving nails at opposing angles makes strong joints (A). A hammer with a narrow cross peen (B) is useful for fine nails.

FIXINGS AND FITTINGS

Most built-in furniture has to be fixed to a wall, ceiling, or floor. It might be possible to make an item so tight in a recess that no attachment is required. Or it might be possible to arrange a part to expand and grip a recess that way. However, in most cases there is a need to fix to the walls if not to the floor or ceiling.

What fastenings you should use depends on the type of wall. If it is wood of sufficient thickness to take screws, attaching the furniture to the wall is no different from screwing any other wood parts together. If it is a substantial piece of furniture or something that will be heavily loaded, it might be necessary to check that the woodwork on the wall is itself sufficiently attached to take this additional load.

Some decorative wood lining can be adequately fixed for its decorative purpose, but it might not be able to take much of a load. If wood is over the studding, screwing through the wood paneling into the studding is desirable.

In any case, use screws that are as long as possible, providing they do not go right through. Because the length of unthreaded neck gets greater as screws get longer, an excessively long screw that goes through might have less grip than one that just spans the thickness (FIG. 3-6). Drill an exploratory hole and check the thickness before settling on the size of screw to use.

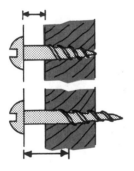

Fig. 3-6. When fixing to wood, a screw of the right length has the better grip.

Attachments to Solid Walls

For solid walls of concrete, brick, stone, or cinder block, it is usually necessary to have some sort of plug into which fastenings can be driven. There are masonry nails, made of hardened steel, that can be driven into many of these surfaces. It is probably best to treat these as locating rather than load-bearing fixings. If the load comes sideways, a nail will grip well enough (FIG. 3-7A); but if the load puts a strain in the direction of withdrawal, it is better to use a screw or some form of through fastening (FIG. 3-7B).

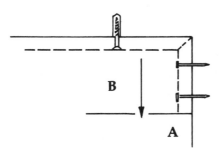

Fig. 3-7. Loads are better taken across a fastening (A) than in the direction it was driven (B).

If masonry is laid with mortar lines, it might be possible to pick or chop out mortar and drive in a wood plug, with the grain across so as to give a screw a good grip. The plug can be given a better hold if it is cut on the skew so it is twisted as it is driven home (FIG. 3-8). For recessed mortar lines use Miller's wedge anchors. These lead anchors are put into the recess in the manner of folding wedges, then the fastening is driven between the wedges.

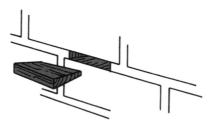

Fig. 3-8. Where screws are needed in a section of masonry, a wood plug can replace chopped out mortar.

With masonry there may be plaster that obscures joints, and fastenings will have to be made at selected places without reference to the location of masonry joints, so holes are more likely to be into solid material than into joints. It is possible to get masonry drills with special tips for drilling stone and other hard materials. They may be used with an ordinary electric drill, but their effectiveness is increased if they are made to vibrate with a percussion action as well as to turn. There are special electric drills for this purpose, or adapters can be obtained for plain drills.

A hole can also be made with a special tool driven with a hammer. The round, fluted tool (star drill) has a diamond-shaped point. It is turned between hammer blows and will penetrate most masonry materials. A careful worker can achieve as good a hole with this tool as with a power drill, but there is more risk of cracks radiating as the hole is made.

When there is a layer of plaster over brick or stone, you should get through this layer with an ordinary drill first before using a masonry drill or a tool with a hammer. If the hole in the plaster is slightly larger than that in the harder material, there is less risk of plaster breaking away (FIG. 3-9A).

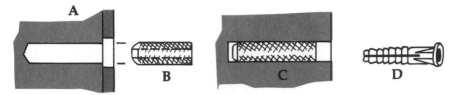

Fig. 3-9. When drilling through a brick wall faced with plaster, make the hole in the outer layer larger than that beneath (A). The plug, preferably a fibrous type (B), should be driven slightly below the surface (C) with a punch; plastic anchor plugs (D) serve the same purpose.

A hold in masonry is obtained by using a plug that expands when a screw is driven. A simple wood plug can be used successfully. This may be roughly rounded so as to make a drive fit in the hole. However, it is better to use a ready-made plug, of which there are several.

A fibrous type (FIG. 3-9B) gives a good grip. When using this type or a wooden plug, consider the screw. If this is only going through a metal plate, part of the unthreaded neck has to go into the wall. If this has to pull its way into the plug at surface level, it might refuse to go or might expand the plug enough to cause the surface of the masonry to break out. It is better to drive the plug a short distance below the surface (FIG. 3-9C) with a punch.

There are plastic anchor plugs which serve the same purpose. Most have a shoulder at surface level and are split so they spread as a screw is driven (FIG. 3-9D). A similar plug made of lead works the same way. For these and other plugs it is important to start with a hole that is a little deeper than the screw is expected to penetrate. The screw cannot be expected to cut its own way farther into the masonry.

Most fastening of built-in furniture with masonry walls will be by wood screws, but where a considerable load has to be taken, you might prefer to use a plug that takes a machine screw. These are threaded so the screw enters easily, but farther down the hole the design is such that further screwing causes the anchor to expand in the hole. Usually the anchor plug comes with a matching screw, perhaps with a choice of heads. For heavy loads a large washer under the head increases its grip (FIG. 3-10A).

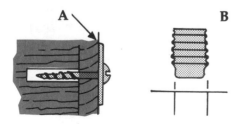

Fig. 3-10. A large washer under the head (A) increases the grip of a screw in an anchor plug. Special plastic plugs are made for chipboard (B).

There are similar plugs for screws into chipboard. Most of these fit ½-inch holes and are made of plastic (FIG. 3-10B). When a screw is driven, the plug expands to grip the hole, but not enough to bulge or burst the chipboard.

Attachments to Hollow Walls

Attachments often have to be made to hollow walls. There are plastic anchors like those for masonry that expand and have gripping ridges around the outside. They can be bought with flanges that will space panels away from the wall (FIG. 3-11A). Such fasteners have a limited grip, but for a piece of furniture that stands on the floor or wherever the load on the fastening is not great, they are convenient.

Other fasteners use machine screws and are designed so that tightening the screw after the plug is inserted causes an expansion on the other side of the panel and prevents withdrawal (FIG. 3-11B).

Another device for fixing to hollow walls involves the use of toggles. The hole has to be large enough to pass the toggle and so is larger than the bolt diameter (FIG. 3-11C). A washer is then needed under the bolt head.

One form of toggle bolt has two spring-loaded arms for the toggle. The arms are pushed through the hole far enough to open then the screw is tightened to pull back against the panel (FIG. 3-11D).

Instead of having a spring, a wing can be weighted or arranged off center (FIG. 3-11E), so gravity causes the inserted assembly to open correctly.

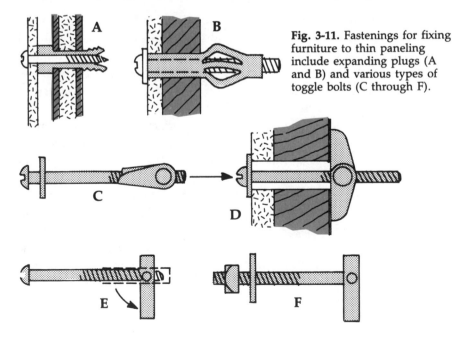

Fig. 3-11. Fastenings for fixing furniture to thin paneling include expanding plugs (A and B) and various types of toggle bolts (C through F).

There may be prongs on the toggle to grip the wall panel. This allows removal and replacement of the bolt without the toggle dropping away.

The bolt does not always go into the toggle. It is sometimes more convenient to have a threaded rod pivoting on a wing and to make the attachment with a nut (FIG. 3-11F).

Locating Fasteners

How many fasteners to use depends on many factors. Much depends on the material to which attachment must be made. Sometimes an attachment does not have the security you expected and additional ones have to be made. A general rule is: never use less than two fastenings. In the case of a hanging bookcase, two well-spread fastenings near the top might be all that are needed. Even then it might be better to have more to spread the load on a lightly built hollow wall.

For larger pieces of furniture, more fixings are needed, particularly up high. How many to use must finally come down to experience, but a spacing of about every foot near the top and every 2 feet near the bottom is reasonable.

Some thought must be given to whether the furniture itself can hold the fixing screws. A piece of plywood or hardboard that forms a back or side panel is not adequate in itself. The screws should go through a strip of solid wood that is part of the framework and properly jointed to other parts.

Plates

Putting a screw through an inch or so of wood is not always easy, particularly if holes have to be made, and plugs inserted, in an awkward place inside a cabinet. In some situations it is preferable to use a metal plate and fix through that. This may be allowed for and built into the furniture, possibly with the plate screwed to a structural part but arranged over a thin panel which is easily accessible (FIG. 3-12A).

Mirrow plates (FIG. 3-12B) are examples of plate mounting which can be made or bought. The name indicates their original use. Two holes are used to screw to the back of the mirror's frame, then the fastening to the wall is made through the remaining hole. For a thing like a bookcase the plates can be arranged less obviously inwards from the sides (FIG. 3-12C).

An alternative that keeps the plate hidden is to make it from thin brass or other metal and give it a double bend. The bending can be done in a vise. After the first bend, a strip of metal is used as a punch to knock the plate back (FIG. 3-12D). There are two screw holes in one arm and a keyhole slot in the other, the latter to hook over a flathead screw projecting from the wall (FIG. 3-12E). Of course, this allows the mirror or other fitting to be removed conveniently for cleaning.

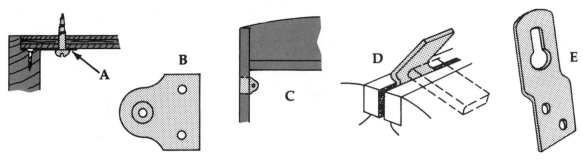

Fig. 3-12. Mounting plates may be bought or made. They can be hidden (A through C) when used for fixing to a wall. A plate with a keyhole slot and a jog can be hidden, yet it allows the furniture to lift off (D and E).

Cabinet Fittings

A great many fittings are available for cabinetwork which are suitable for built-in furniture. There is little standardization, and the range of fittings available in one place may be different from those elsewhere. As some of these things—special hinges, catches for doors, brackets for flaps, and so on—are designed for wood of certain thicknesses or for particular movements, be sure to check on the availability of suitable fittings before getting too far into the design and construction of a piece of furniture. This will be much better than trying to alter something already made to suit the only available fittings.

Hinges. Ordinary hinges are dealt with in Chapter 4, and these should be used in any piece of built-in furniture of traditional pattern. For modern applications there are now hundreds of different styles available. If you anticipate a special hinge problem in a piece of furniture, check out the available types before going ahead with the work.

If a door is to overlap, it can have a *cranked* hinge (FIG. 3-13A). These can be bought plated and with decorative outline shapes, and they are attractive on kitchen and bathroom cabinets. Some of the thickness of a butt hinge can be removed by making the two parts so one fits into a space in the other (FIG. 3-13B). The whole hinge is then probably no thicker than the clearance that will be given the door, and there is no need to recess it. There are also *cranked flush* hinges (FIG. 3-13C). A *double-cranked flush* hinge throws the door clear (FIG. 3-13D).

Many hinges are available that are similar to those on car doors, where linkage is used to swing the door clear as it opens. Some of these seem unnecessarily complicated for most built-in furniture, but if there is a need for a door to swing around an obstruction, there is probably a hinge made that will do it.

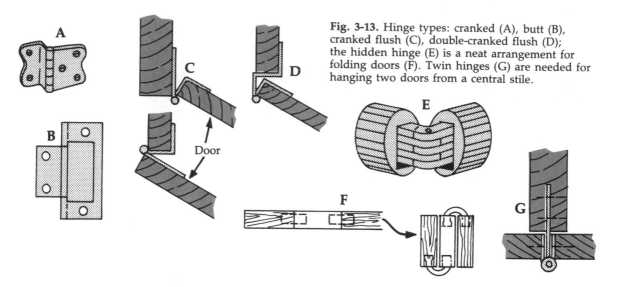

Fig. 3-13. Hinge types: cranked (A), butt (B), cranked flush (C), double-cranked flush (D); the hidden hinge (E) is a neat arrangement for folding doors (F). Twin hinges (G) are needed for hanging two doors from a central stile.

In some modern furniture the hinges are hidden when the door or lid is closed. In one type the two halves are circular and fit into holes (FIG. 3-13E). The hinges have a locking arranged to keep them in the holes. These hinges can be used to make neat folding doors (FIG. 3-13F).

If you want to hang two doors from a central stile, one option is twin hinges (FIG. 3-13G). The central tongue fits into a slot. The doors may open to 90 degrees together, or one door may swing fully back over the other closed one.

Catches. Doors and lids have to be fastened and they need handles. Sometimes the means of fastening is incorporated in a handle. What is used depends on the piece of furniture. There are styles applicable to traditional, colonial, and modern pieces.

Magnetic catches are convenient, as they need no action other than a pull to release. They are in several forms, but all incorporate on one part and a magnet and iron plate to attract it on the other part (FIG. 3-14A).

Another catch uses a roller under spring pressure (FIG. 3-14B). Related to these are the ball catches (FIG. 3-14C and D).

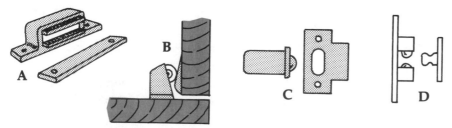

Fig. 3-14. Catches for doors and lids: magnetic catch (A), roller catch (B), ball catches (C and D).

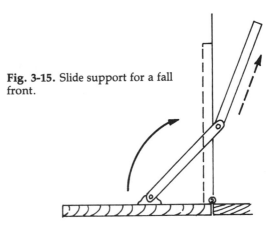

Fig. 3-15. Slide support for a fall front.

A common construction in built-in furniture is a *fall front*, which serves as a writing surface or a kitchen working surface. Although two or more ordinary hinges could be used, this is a place for a piano hinge—a continuous length of hinge which is cut to length and screwed at intervals.

The fall front has to be supported in some way. In some traditional furniture there were pullout supports below, but today stays are more common. An arm with a bracket is affixed to the flap, and the other end is on a slide. At the bottom of the slide its movement is stopped at the point where the flap has reached the correct position (FIG. 3-15). There are many variations on this principle.

Handles. Handles for cabinetwork come in an infinite number of patterns in wood, metal, and plastic. A handle may be fastened from the front (FIG. 3-16A) or back (FIG. 3-16B). A drawer pull differs from a door pull by usually allowing the fingers to go underneath (FIG. 3-16C). Other handles may go on the edge (FIG. 3-16D). Sometimes handles can be dispensed with by providing holes or notches (FIG. 3-16E). A further step is an inset metal finger-pull (FIG. 3-16F).

Period furniture can inspire ideas for many knobs and handles, as well as modern designs. Be sure to take into account everything that will be around the particular piece. Handles have to be compatible with their surroundings.

Making your own handles can be very rewarding. If you have a lathe, turned knobs are interesting projects. Handles do not have to be very ornate. Drawer pulls can be made in a long piece and cut off (FIG. 3-16G). Door handles can be made in a similar way. If the same wood as the rest of the construction is used and you want to add some color include a piece of Plexiglass under the handle. This will also prevent the wood from becoming soiled.

Other Fittings. Although the enthusiastic woodworker will want to make and fit drawers by traditional methods, several drawer slide

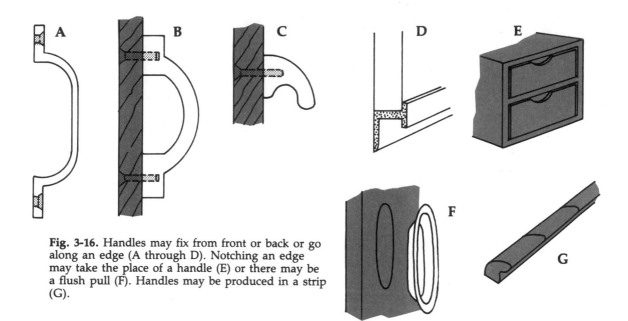

Fig. 3-16. Handles may fix from front or back or go along an edge (A through D). Notching an edge may take the place of a handle (E) or there may be a flush pull (F). Handles may be produced in a strip (G).

assemblies can be obtained. They often provide a smoother action than wood sliding on wood, and some provide a much better support when the drawer is fully drawn.

Doors do not always have to swing; it might be more convenient to have them slide. There are several types of sliding-door gear in cabinet sizes. If you use one, buy it first so the piece of furniture can be designed to suit it.

Though proper cabinetmaking joints should always be used where possible, there are places where reinforcement may be advisable or where a simple piece of hardware could give added strength to a joint. This sometimes happens when more than two pieces of wood meet in one place and the joint cut results in quite a lot of wood being removed from each piece. There are flat plates (FIG. 3-17A), corner plates (FIG. 3-17B), and others shaped like brackets to go around inside or outside of corners (FIG. 3-17C).

Shelves may be supported in other parts of the woodwork at their ends, but if intermediate supports are needed or the shelf has to be supported without benefit of framing, metal shelf brackets (FIG. 3-17D) are neater and less obvious than any wooden brackets. If there is a possibility the shelves will later be moved, use adjustable brackets.

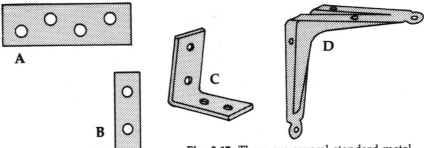

Fig. 3-17. There are several standard metal reinforcing plates (A through C) besides shelf brackets (D).

4

Joints

JOINTS IN WOODWORK provide strength by the overlapping and interlocking of parts. Sometimes the joint produces strength by the combination of grains in different directions.

GLUED AND LAPPED JOINTS

Glue grips best on the side of the grain. The grip directly on end grain may be very slight, so joints are designed to bring meeting surfaces together either with the grain or at a shallow angle to it. Wood joints are made to give good glue area for maximum adhesion. The only joints that are not glued are those which use wedges or keys, as in some garden furniture and traditional pieces and in those items which may have to be dismantled.

Making Panels

The width of a board obviously cannot be more than the thickness of the tree from which it was cut. At one time much furniture making involved the building up of boards to width, and some paneled furniture of earlier days was designed that way as much to avoid wide boards as for the sake of appearance.

With plywood and the many other forms of manufactured built-up boards, many of the problems of wide panels can be avoided. The range of sheet material with veneers and other surface finishes is such that pieces up to any usual furniture width can be found to match the solid wood elsewhere in the piece. For new work these wide materials are usually chosen, but there are many places, even in new construction, where edge-to-edge joints have to be made, and there are several points to watch.

It is inadvisable to glue two machine-planed edges without other preparation. The action of machine planing, particularly if the cutters are not perfectly sharp, "casehardens" the surface so that it resists the penetration of glue. The edges should be hand-planed—not sanded. Any form of sanding tends to round the angles, and this is undesirable.

Difficulty in these joints often comes at the ends, where the pieces may tend to spring apart and open the joint. This can be obviated by planing the edges very slightly hollow. A bar clamp across the middle will then pull the whole joint close (FIG. 4-1A). *Joiner's dogs* are also useful for pulling ends close (FIG. 4-1B). Their inner tapered legs give a wedge action as they are driven.

Fig. 4-1. Dogs provide a simple way of holding board edges together.

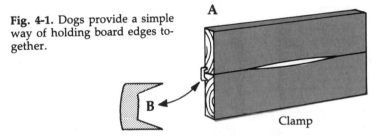

If wood warps, the tendency is for annual rings to straighten. If several boards are to be joined to make up a width, it is good practice to examine the ends and arrange the curves of annual rings in alternate directions (FIG. 4-2). Little warping can be expected from properly seasoned furniture woods, but if it does occur, overall distortion will be minimized.

Fig. 4-2. Having grain opposite ways reduces the risk of overall warping.

A system called *secret slot screwing* can be used to pull glued edges together without clamps and impart some cross-grain strength. This is particularly useful when a very long joint is being made, as the screws also keep the boards in the same plane. Screws driven into one board have to mate with slots in the other. How many are used along a joint depends on the wood and its thickness, but a spacing of 6 inches in softwood 1 inch thick, or 12 inches in hardwood, is reasonable.

Mark the centers on both pieces, then the piece which will not have the screws driven into it has additional marks made, two to three times

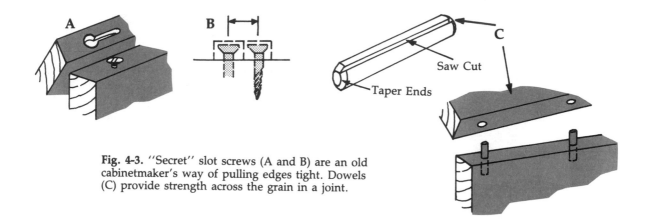

Fig. 4-3. "Secret" slot screws (A and B) are an old cabinetmaker's way of pulling edges tight. Dowels (C) provide strength across the grain in a joint.

the diameter of the screw head from the first. Screws are driven until the threads are buried. In the opposite piece there is a hole to clear the screw head, taken a little deeper than the screw projects, and a slot alongside it wide enough to clear the shank of the screw (FIG. 4-3A).

The boards are brought together dry, and the screws are inserted in their opposite holes; then one board is driven along the other so the screw heads cut along the grain (FIG. 4-3B). If this test assembly is satisfactory, the joint is knocked apart and the screws each are given a quarter turn. Glue is applied and the joints driven together again.

Another way of strengthening and securing a glued joint is to have dowels across it at intervals (FIG. 4-3C). The dowels should be about one-third the thickness of the wood. Careful marking and straight drilling will make a good joint. If possible, drill with an electric drill in a stand. There can be a bursting action when a dowel goes into its hole like a piston into a cylinder if air and surplus glue cannot escape. Making a saw cut along the dowel gives a safety groove.

Lap Joints

When two pieces of wood have to cross or meet and the surfaces have to be flush, the simplest joint is a *lap* joint. There are many variations. In the basic cross lap (FIG. 4-4A), both parts are the same size. The same joint may be a corner or end lap (FIG. 4-4B), or a middle lap (FIG. 4-4C) at a T-junction. The parts are not always the same width or thickness, or flush, or at a right angle.

In general you should not cut away more than half the thickness of the thinner part. The parts to be joined should be marked from the face surfaces and the widths of cuts should be obtained from the actual pieces (FIG. 4-4D). Use a marking gauge from the face side on both pieces. All

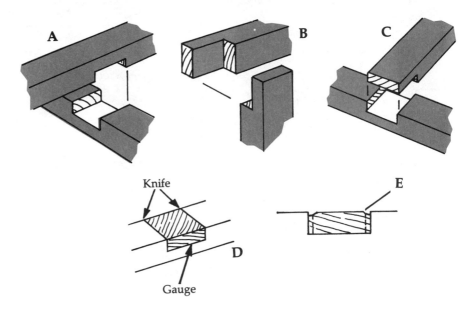

Fig. 4-4. Lap joints cross lap (A), corner or end lap (B), middle lap (C). The widths of the cuts are taken from the pieces (D); the one to be inset is beveled with a chisel (E).

other lines are best made with a knife so as to sever the fibers and allow a clean cut with the saw.

Mark the waste parts to prevent mistakes. Saw cuts have to be made on the waste sides of the lines. To prevent the saw carrying its kerf over the line, bevel on the waste side of the knife-cut line with a chisel (FIG. 4-4E) as a guide for the start of the saw cut.

Making the Cut. With the wood in the vise or against the bench hook, use a fine backsaw. To avoid going too deep, tilt the saw forward until it is down to the line on the far side, then back until the near side is reached. Finally make a few light strokes horizontally until the depth is the same right through.

In many cases no other sawing is needed; but if the wood is very wide, intermediate cuts can be made in the waste part to ease its removal by chiseling. Although a small circular saw would have the benefit of controlling the depth of cut, getting the saw exactly on the line for a precision cut is difficult, so it is usually better to make lap joints by hand.

With the wood in the vise use a board chisel to pare diagonally into the joint (FIG. 4-5). Follow the gauge line very closely, then turn the wood around and do the same from the other side. Finally pare straight across. Check that the bottom of the cut is level. A slight hollowing tendency is less noticeable a flaw than for the bottom to be higher in the middle.

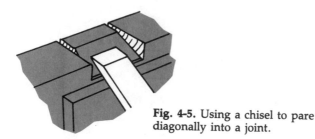

Fig. 4-5. Using a chisel to pare diagonally into a joint.

Where one part is the end of a piece of wood, it can be sawn completely. Marking is the same as for a cross lap, but I suggest you leave a little extra on the end to be planed after assembly (FIG. 4-6A).

After making the cross-grained cut, hold the wood in the vise at a slight angle. Saw diagonally on the waste side of the gauge line, watching progress of the kerf across the end and down the side (FIG. 4-6B). Turn the wood over and do the same the other way (FIG. 4-6C), and then cut straight through (FIG. 4-6D). After a little practice a satisfactory result will be obtained simply from the saw; but if necessary, the meeting surface can be trimmed with a chisel.

This cut can be made on a table saw, providing the wood is not so long as to be unwieldy and the depth of cut is no more than the projection of the saw blade. The wood is traversed over the saw at the right depth setting, against the fence set to the final thickness. In the usual right-angled joint, the wood has to be kept upright, and a push piece with a square corner is helpful (FIG. 4-7).

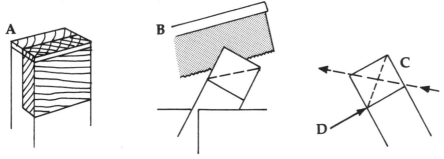

Fig. 4-6. Cutting joint parts with a backsaw.

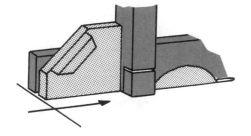

Fig. 4-7. Parts for a right-angled joint must be kept upright when they are being cut on a table saw.

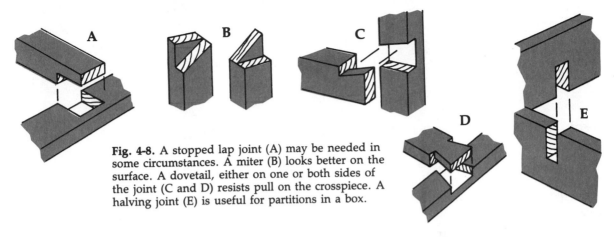

Fig. 4-8. A stopped lap joint (A) may be needed in some circumstances. A miter (B) looks better on the surface. A dovetail, either on one or both sides of the joint (C and D) resists pull on the crosspiece. A halving joint (E) is useful for partitions in a box.

The tool techniques involved in making lap joints occur in many other joints, so lap or halving construction forms a good introduction to the making of other joints.

Variations of Lap Joint. Some variations of the simple lap joint include a *stopped* lap joint, where it would spoil the appearance of an edge if the end grain of the T-piece showed through (FIG. 4-8A). If a corner would look better with a miter showing on the face side, the *halving* joint can be adopted (FIG. 4-8B), but this joint is not as strong as a full lap joint.

If the load taken tends to pull on the joint, use a *dovetail* form for either one (FIG. 4-8C) or both (FIG. 4-8D) sides of the joint. This can be combined with a stopped lap joint. A halving joint can be made edgewise on the wood, (FIG. 4-8E) to form partitions in a box.

TENON AND DOWEL JOINTS

The greatest integral strength, as distinct from any strength glue may contribute, comes in joints in which one part fits into another rather than resting on it or being recessed into a side. There are many places where other joints are more appropriate, but the joints most used in furniture of framed construction are those in which a piece projecting from one part fits into a socket in another piece. When the projecting piece is part of the solid wood, it is a *tenon*, and the socket it fits into is a *mortise*.

Although dowels had some use in traditional furniture, they get much greater use today, as power tools make them easier to use with accuracy for joints that would otherwise have been tenoned.

Mortise And Tenon Joints

In the basic mortise and tenon joint between two pieces at right angles (FIG. 4-9) the tenon is usually about one-third the width of the wood on which it is cut. This applies when the other piece is the same or a similar

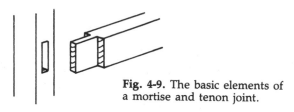

Fig. 4-9. The basic elements of a mortise and tenon joint.

width. If the other piece is much wider, you will achieve greater strength in the joint if you do not cut away as much from the tenoned piece.

Although it is unusual to chop out mortises completely with a chisel, you will have to use a chisel for trimming. Always make the tenon and mortise to match the chisel rather than a measurement obtained from a rule.

Allow a little extra on the end of the tenoned piece if it is to go right through; you can plane it flush later. Cut around the shoulders with a knife and use a mortise gauge to mark the tenon (FIG. 4-10A). On the other piece, mark the mortise limits with pencil and carry them around to the other side with a try square down the face surface. Mark the width of the mortise on both sides with the gauge (FIG. 4-10B). Saw away the waste on each side of the tenon as described for a sawn lap joint (FIGS. 4-6 and 4-7).

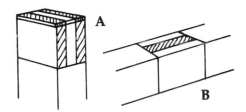

Fig. 4-10. In its simplest form the mortise and tenon joint is one-third the thickness of the pieces joined.

To make the mortise with a chisel only, support the wood on the bench (not in the vise, where grain on the far side might break out). Then use a chisel of the same width as the mortise along with a mallet and chop centrally, making further cuts towards the ends, but not right up to them (FIG. 4-11A). Use the same chisel, or a narrower one, to hook out the waste.

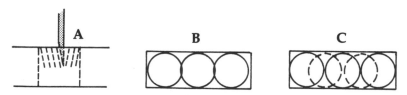

Fig. 4-11. A mortise and tenon joint may be chopped out (A). Overlapping drilled holes will remove most of the waste (B and C).

Repeat process if necessary, until the cut reaches halfway. Then turn the wood over and repeat from the other side. Finally, with the chisel, pare down to the line at each end of the mortise. Then clamp and glue.

Use an electric drill, either freehand or in a stand, to remove most of the waste. You can use a slightly undersize drill to make holes that just touch the mortise edges and leave little wood to be removed with a chisel (FIG. 4-11B) In another method a guide is used for the drill. The guide is fed into intermediate positions between the first row of holes and leaves extremely little waste to be removed. If the strip of wood can be moved along a guide piece, the drill itself can remove the remaining waste, leaving only the ends of the mortise to be squared with a chisel (FIG. 4-11C).

Another way is to use a router, which enters the wood and then moves sideways to cut the slot. To do this accurately, the wood must be locked in a slide which traverses the wood correctly in relation to the cutter.

Professional mortising is often done with a special hollow chisel. This is square and sharpened on the inside. An auger turns in its center. This combination is lowered into the wood, and the chisel pares downward as the auger removes waste (FIG. 4-12A). The mortise is made by working a series of squares. There are accessories for some electric drills which allow this method to be used in a home shop.

In some constructions a dowel may be put through the joint. This is valuable in a place where clamping is difficult or impossible. The hole in the tenon is staggered slightly from that in the mortised piece so that driving in a dowel with a tapered end pulls the joint together (FIG. 4-12B). In some traditional and any takedown furniture, the tenon is made long enough to leave a tusk to take a wedge or key (FIG. 4-12C), which pulls the joint tight and holds it.

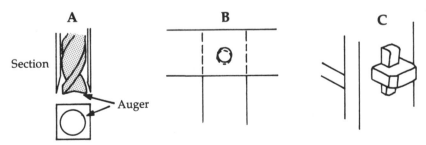

Fig. 4-12. A special hollow tool can be used in a power drill (A) to remove the waste in a mortise made with overlapping holes. A peg through staggered holes (B) will pull a tenon into its mortise. Wedges through extended tenons (C) are found in some traditional furniture.

Other Mortise and Tenon Joints. If the tenon would be unsightly if taken right through, as in a rail to a leg, a *stub (blind)* tenon is used (FIG. 4-13A). You should have no difficulty making this joint except in getting

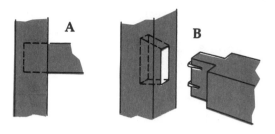

Fig. 4-13. Variations on the mortise and tenon joint include one that uses a stub, or blind, tenon (A) and one made extra secure by fox wedging (B).

the depth of the mortise right. Ideally the tenon should touch bottom as the shoulders meet the surface, but since it is more important for appearance that the shoulders are tight, you can cut the mortise a little deeper.

It is possible to make this joint extra firm by *fox-wedging*: the inside of the mortise tapers outward slightly at the ends, then wedges in saw cuts in the tenon spread it as it is driven home (FIG. 4-13B). Wedges are sometimes used with through tenons, but this is more common in doors and house construction than in furniture making.

If two rails meet in a log, the ends can be mitered to allow the maximum lengths of tenons (FIG. 4-14A). If one surface of the tenoned piece is to come level with the surface of the other piece, it can be *barefaced* (FIG. 4-14B). This is also useful for a rail that is not very thick. A shoulder cut in both sides might leave little strength in the remaining wood in the tenon. A second advantage in having only one shoulder to cut is that it will pull close. If the two shoulders are not cut exactly the same, however, one side might not be as good a fit as the other.

When the joint comes at a corner, it can be an open, or *bridle*, joint (FIG. 4-14C). Although this joint may have some uses in carpentry, it is uncommon in furniture construction. It is more common to cut the tenon back to make a *haunched* mortise and tenon joint (FIG. 4-14D). The tapered haunch does not show at the end. Be sure to leave some waste on the end of the mortised piece and do not remove this until after the joint has been glued. Doing so reduces any risk of the end grain breaking out as the mortise is cut or the joint assembled. If the framing includes a panel recessed into grooves, cut the tenon back to the bottom of the groove, and square the haunch to fit the groove in the other piece (FIG. 4-14E).

Special Large Joints. If the piece to be tenoned is very wide, the mortise to take a large single tenon might weaken the mortised piece. In that case there can be two parts to the tenon, with or without a short piece between (FIG. 4-15A). If the tenoned part is very thick, two tenons (FIG. 4-15B) might be better than a single thick one. If the boards to be joined are very wide, use a large number of pins spaced at intervals about the same width as the pins. If the pins have diagonal saw cuts made in them before assembly, they can be tightened with glued wedges (FIG. 4-15C).

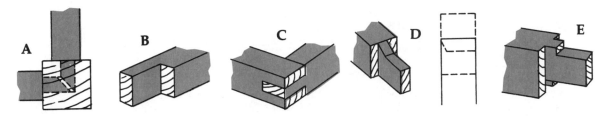

Fig. 4-14. Tenons on rails can be made to meet within the joint by mitering their ends (A); the barefaced tenon is often used on rails that aren't very thick. Corners may show parts (C), or be stopped (D and E).

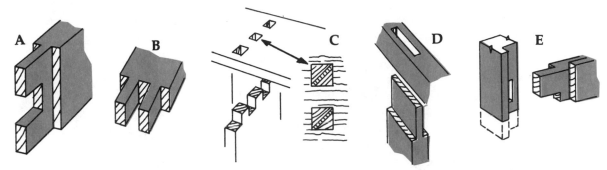

Fig. 4-15. Where the wood is wide or shaped, you can use the special joints shown.

If mortise and tenon joints are not at right angles, they should be designed so that shaping the tenons does not cut across lines of grain, even if this means entering at an angle (FIG. 4-15D). Breaking through grain weakens the wood.

The mortise and tenon principle can be adapted to many types of assembly. For instance, a piece tenoned into another with a rabbet can have long and short shoulders (FIG. 4-15E), which will look better than if you cut away the other part to allow both shoulders to be in the same plane.

Doweling

Traditionally, craftsmen made dowels as they needed them. Today it is more usual to buy machine-made dowel rods in various woods and in many lengths and diameters. Not all wood is suitable for manufacture in this way, however, so if a particular wood is needed, the craftsman may still make his own. Some oak furniture, for instance, looks best with the ends of dowels exposed at joints. These should be oak, but is is unlikely that you'll find ready-made lengths.

Dowels can be made on a lathe, but they are more readily made with a *dowel plate* (FIG. 4-16A), which is merely a stout drilled steel plate, used over a vise or mounted on a block of wood. The holes may taper, but plain drilled ones will also work.

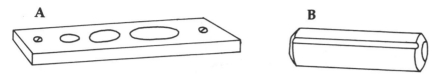

Fig. 4-16. Dowels can be made by knocking wood through holes in a plate (A). A groove along a dowel allows air and surplus glue to escape (B).

Plane the wood square, then plane the corners off. Now chisel a rough taper on one end, then drive the stick through the plate. Dowels are best made this way, only slightly longer than the length needed for one dowel.

Dowels, whether homemade or cut from a length, should be tapered slightly at the ends and grooved (FIG. 4-16B) to allow air and excess glue to escape. The main problem in doweling is obtaining squareness in mating pieces. The use of an electric drill in a stand helps, but not all assemblies can be held this way. There are doweling jigs that clamp to the wood and guide the drill squarely to the surface. If much doweling is to be done, such a jig is essential for consistently good work.

If drilling has to be done without any mechanical aid to control direction, the wood should be secured, and a hollow should be made where the drill is to enter, either with a spike or a punch. It is useful to have an assistant view the drill, but if you are working alone, stand one or more squares nearby as guides.

Some doweling jigs help in spacing dowel holes on the parts to be joined. In any case the holes must be marked accurately. The need for this becomes more acute as the number of dowels in a joint increases. One slightly incorrect dowel is enough to prevent proper assembly. In some joints it is possible to use a template on both pieces (FIG. 4-17) or make a jig with pointed nails to mark both surfaces.

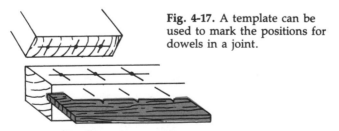

Fig. 4-17. A template can be used to mark the positions for dowels in a joint.

There is no standard way of deciding on the size and spacing of dowels; it depends on experience. Diameters should not usually be as much as half the thickness of the wood, and the space between the edges of holes is usually greater than the dowel diameter. To keep parts correctly registered in relation to each other, use at least two dowels per joint (FIG. 4-18A).

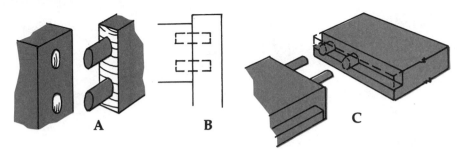

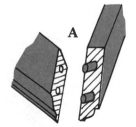
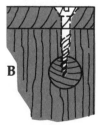

Fig. 4-18. At least two dowels are needed to keep joint parts properly aligned (A); they should project into the mating parts by the same amount (B). When dowels are used instead of a tenon in a joint with a rabbet, the holes for them should be drilled before the rabbet is cut (C).

Dowels do not usually go right through. The amount of projection in a framed structure might be about three-quarters of the thickness of the wood. It is best to go about the same distance into each piece (FIG. 4-18B).

In certain situations you should drill for dowels before other work has been finished. For instance, if you want to join two rabbeted parts and you are using dowels(FIG. 4-18C), drill the holes before the rabbets are made; afterwards it would be almost impossible to do accurately.

Dowels strengthen joints where end grains meet and glue would not provide a good grip, yet an elaborate joint is not justified. A mitered corner between pieces that add decoration more than strength on the top of a high cabinet is an example (FIG. 4-9A). The dowels must be at right angles to the surfaces that meet, unlike tenons, which have to follow grain lines.

Screws do not hold well in end grain, but dowels can be used to provide extra grip (FIG. 4-19B). The dowel should be far enough down for there to be no risk of the end grain fracturing under the pull of the screw on the dowel, and the screw should be long enough to go almost through the dowel.

Fig. 4-19. Dowels can help glue get a grip on the end grain of mitered corner pieces (A). They can also be used to provide a grip for a screw in end grain (B).

DOVETAIL JOINTS

If any one family of joints can be regarded as the mark of fine cabinetwork, it is the dovetail. The tenon flared causes resistance from pulling apart

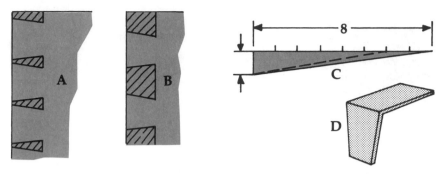

Fig. 4-20. Dovetails are found in most traditional furniture and are considered the mark of good craftsmanship. Handmade dovetails have narrow pins (A), but machine made dovetails have parts of equal width (B). The taper ratio of dovetail sides is usually 1:8 (C); a piece of bent metal serves as a guide to its shape (D).

in one direction, whether or not glue or metal fastenings are also used. The design of dovetails varies. Old-time craftsmen were very proud of making the joints with extremely narrow pins between the dovetails (FIG. 4-20A). This was certainly a sign of their skill, but the joints could not have been as strong as if the pins had been made wider. At the other extreme are machine-made dovetails, which are quite satisfactory; but the pins and dovetails are the same width (FIG. 4-20B). Hand-cut dovetails are probably best kept to sizes between the two extremes.

The taper ratio of the sides of the dovetails is usually about 1:8 (FIG. 4-20C). This suits most hardwoods. Softwoods might be broadened slightly, but the ratio should not be less than 1:6. A piece of thin sheet metal may be bent and filed for use as a template (FIG. 4-20D).

Through Dovetails

A through dovetail joint may be the single kind (FIG. 21-A) or the multiple kind (FIG. 4-21B). It might take a little experimenting to get an even

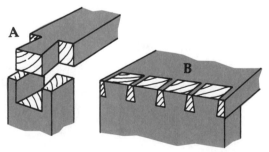

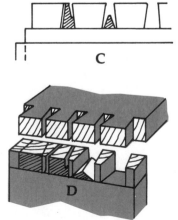

Fig. 4-21. Through dovetails, joints may be single or multiple (A and B). Much of the waste can be sawn from one part, then this can be used to mark the other part (C and D).

spacing. The joint may be cut by hand, dovetails first or pins first. To cut the dovetail piece first, mount the wood in a vise and saw down the sides of the dovetail with a backsaw on the waste side of the lines (FIG. 4-21C). Chop out the remaining waste with a bevel-edged chisel, working a little from each side on the bench. Then use the chisel to pare back to the line.

With the other piece in the vise and the depth marked all around, put the dovetail piece in position, and use a fine pencil point or a sharp awl to mark the shapes on the end. Then square down to the line (FIG. 4-21D).

Be careful to saw on the waste side of the lines. Some of the waste can be removed by diagonal saw cuts. In large joints, drill a series of holes across the waste or use a scroll saw to cut most of it away.

Final trimming is done with a chisel, but be careful of damaging the tapered sides of the pins. If cutting pins first is favored, marking one from the other is in a different sequence, but otherwise the cutting is the same.

A craftsman prefers not to make a trial assembly, although this might be best for a beginner. Check that the bottoms of the cuts are in line and flat across the thickness of the wood. A trial assembly tends to loosen the joint, so if you trust your judgement and workmanship, apply glue and make the first assembly the last.

Concealed Joints

In some furniture, exposed joints are regarded as a desirable feature, but elsewhere it is better if the joints are concealed, at least in one direction. In a drawer, for example, the dovetails should not show on the front. This is accomplished by a *stopped* or *blind* dovetail joint (FIG. 4-22A).

The dovetails are marked and cut in the same way as for a through dovetail, but they should only be long enough to go part way across the other piece. How far across depends on the total thickness, but there must be enough material left to resist breaking out during the chopping operation.

The depth is marked on the second piece, which is held in the vise while the dovetail shapes are drawn on it. A gauge line will ensure even depth. Not much can be sawn away, but a fine backsaw can be used to cut diagonally as far as possible on the waste side of each line, then some cuts can be made in the waste (FIG. 4-22B). The rest of the waste has to be removed by chisel, cutting across the grain before slicing along it (FIG. 4-22C). Have the wood supported on a bench top or other solid surface and be careful not to go too deep with the chisel.

The dovetails can be hidden in both directions if you use a *stopped lap* dovetail joint. A narrow edge still shows (FIG. 4-22D). One place where this is used is in the corner of a plinth under a cabinet.

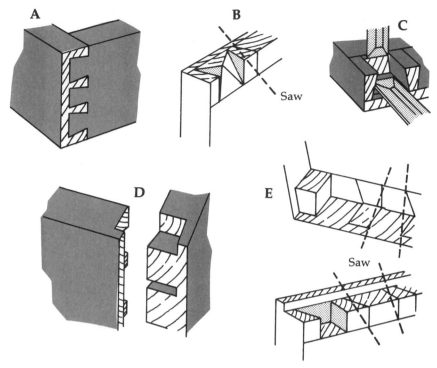

Fig. 4-22. In drawers and similar constructions, dovetail joints are stopped so the construction is hidden in one direction.

The pattern of the joint being marked may be thought of as a blind dovetail joint with a flap over the second layer of end grain. It is like a through dovetail with an extra thickness on the outside of both pieces to be joined.

Prepare the wood by cutting back the piece that is to overlap (FIG. 4-22E). It does not matter which piece carries the dovetails; it depends on which way the resistance to pull is to come in relation to the narrow piece of exposed end grain.

Mark the thickness of the part of the other piece that is to be jointed on both pieces and outline the dovetails. Cut these as far as possible by sawing. Most of the work will be careful chopping and paring with a chisel. Mark the second piece from the first and cut it similarly.

Mitered Dovetail. The ultimate in hand dovetailing is a mitered dovetail, in which no sign of the joint is visible (FIG. 4-23A). This may be thought of as a through dovetail with an extra thickness on both pieces. Both parts are prepared by cutting back the amount that will be mitered, but it is safer not to plane or chisel the miters at this stage. It might be difficult keeping the saw or chisel from going farther than intended when cutting the dovetails and pins, but this will not matter if it only goes into the

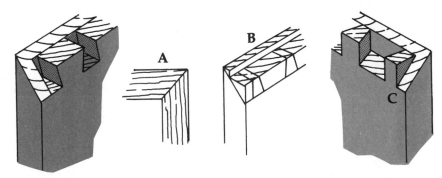

Fig. 4-23. In a mitered dovetail, construction is hidden.

waste that is yet to be removed (FIG. 4-23B). In some work it will not matter if the miter does not extend across the thickness of the wood, as this will be hidden; but if the edge will be exposed in the finished construction, allow for mitering the edges (FIG. 4-23C).

Cutting is similar to that for stopped and lapped joints. When the dovetail parts are completed, the miter can be trimmed with a paring chisel. A shoulder plane is a good tool for final leveling.

Other Dovetail Joints. Several devices are available for making dovetails by machine. For home use there is an arrangement that clamps the wood and acts as a template for a rotary router, which can be driven by an electric drill or other power source. The method gives automatic accuracy and spacing, usually with pins and dovetails the same width (FIG. 4-24A). The rounded ends may seem less satisfactory than squared corners, but in practice, the joints are satisfactory.

If dovetailing is to be used where parts meet obliquely, the angles of the dovetails should be related to the lines of grain (FIG. 4-24B) in the same way as mortise and tenon joints meet. If a drawer side is to be grooved for a plywood bottom, the bottom half-dovetail can be made wide enough to take the groove and hide it in the joint (FIG. 4-24C).

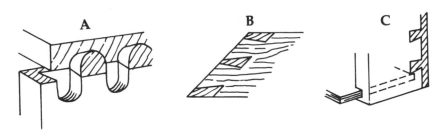

Fig. 4-24. The parts of machine dovetails are cut together (A). Where corners are not square, the dovetail angles are kept in line (B). The bottom of a drawer can be hidden in the bottom dovetail (C).

If a construction is to be made in box form, it is better to make the lid and box in one piece and saw them apart rather than to try to get two separate constructions to match.

Where one part of a joint has to fit into another so its ends are buried, it must be cut to exact length. Where a part goes through, you can leave a little waste to be planed later. Make sure not to leave too much on the part with dovetails, however, or it will interfere with removing the waste wood.

It is often possible to mark out and saw several dovetailed ends, such as a batch of drawer sides, while they are held together in a vise. Except for the front piece, which has to be detailed, marking is then restricted to depth lines on each piece and lines squared across the adjoining ends.

DADO AND OTHER JOINTS

When a piece like a shelf has to be supported by an upright, it is usually recessed into a groove, which is the basic *dado* or *housing* joint.

Types of Dado Joints

How much to cut out for the dado depends on the thickness of the wood. Too much must not be taken out, or the wood will be weakened; but the groove must be deep enough to support the other piece (FIG. 4-25).

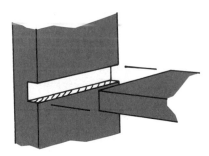

Fig. 4-25. This type of dado joint is visible from both sides of the upright.

The dado can be cut in much the same way as described for making lap joints, but the cuts are longer. If you have doubt about being able to control the saw on a wide board, clamp on a piece of straight wood as a guide. With a suitable traveling guide, it might be possible to make the cut with a table saw; however, it is easier to make the cut accurate with a radial arm saw. A wobble saw or a dado head is more appropriate to cuts with the grain, but leaves a ragged edge when used.

This is the joint where the old-woman's-tooth type of hand router is used to level the bottom of the groove after most of the waste has been removed with a chisel. A power router can be used to remove the waste and will leave a smooth bottom.

Stopped Dado. In bookcase construction it is better if the front of the groove does not show, so a stopped dado is used (FIG. 4-26A). The piece at the front that is not cut is kept to a minimum: ¼ inch is about right. Make sure the forward part of the cut on the shelf is neat by using a knife to mark the edge deeply, and bevel against this with a chisel before sawing.

If you want to cut the stopped dado completely by hand, chop out to the full width and depth near the closed end, but leave a little spare in the length of the groove (FIG. 4-26B). How much is cut in this way depends on the craftsman, but about an inch will do. This is to allow movement of the saw in a pared groove against the cut line (FIG. 4-26C). The saw will probably hit the end of the slot, but this will not matter if there is a little waste left there to be removed as a final step. Remove any waste with a chisel and router.

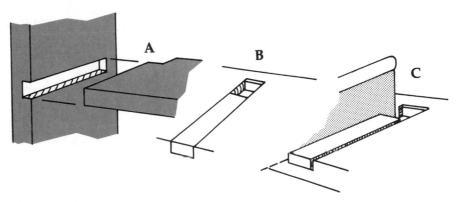

Fig. 4-26. The stopped dado joint (A) is ideally suited, for appearances, to bookcase construction. Paring out about an inch of the groove at the closed end of the groove (B) makes room for saw movement later (C).

Dadoes for Extra Strength. In the ordinary dado joint the side grain is brought against end grain, which is not very satisfactory for gluing. This does not matter in many constructions, where other parts of the assembly relieve the dado joints of much strain; but where extra strength is necessary, there are ways of strengthening. A fillet of wood can be glued in the angle underneath (FIG. 4-27A), or screws can be driven inconspicuously from below (FIG. 4-27B).

The joint can also be strengthened by giving it a dovetail form on one or both edges (FIG. 4-27C). This entails sawing the sides of the dado carefully, with the saw at the correct angle. As with other dovetails, a taper ratio of 1:8 is about right. The shelf cut should be deeply scored-in with a knife, and the bevel should be started with a chisel. In smaller

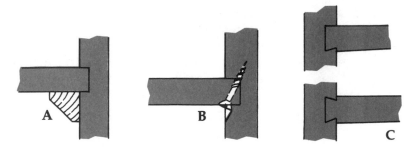

Fig. 4-27. Two methods of giving added support to the crossmember of a dado are the use of a fillet (A) and screws (B). Extra strength can be given to the joint by making it take a dovetail form (C).

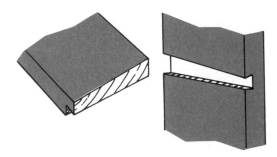

Fig. 4-28. In a tapered dovetail dado the parts are wedged together.

work there may be no need for sawing. It is usually sufficient to dovetail only one edge.

A further step that gives utmost closeness of joint and the greatest resistance to pulling the shelf from the groove involves making a dovetail joint, with another taper in the width of the shelf. Much taper is difficult to give in thin shelves, but the tapered dovetail dado has considerable strength in thicker wood, whether stopped at the front or taken right through (FIG. 4-28). Assemble by driving the shelf in from the back. One advantage of this joint is that it locks both pieces to shape, and therefore, will be wrap-resistant.

Miters

A miter joint is usually thought of as being at 45 degrees in a 90-degree corner (FIG. 4-29A), but it could be at other angles. In fact, even in a 90-degree corner, two parts of different width necessitate a different angle of cut (FIG. 4-29B). Unusual joints should be laid out carefully, full size, to get the angles. With a 45-degree miter, a square may be drawn and its diagonal used to give the setting for an adjustable bevel if a miter square or suitable combination square is unavailable. The simplest miter is a plain cut, as in the corner of a picture frame (FIG. 4-29C).

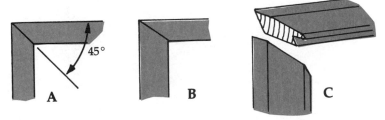

Fig. 4-29. Where parts meet, the neatest joint on the surface is a miter, which is 45° if the parts are the same width (A), but another angle (B) if they are different. The simplest miter is a plain cut (C).

Tools and Techniques for Mitering. Although the ends might be cut to fit exactly with no more than the usual bench tools, there are devices that facilitate fast, accurate cutting. A miter box (FIG. 4-30A) provides a guide for a backsaw. A more elaborate metal guide uses the same principle with more precision. Planing can be done on a special shuting board (FIG. 4-30B).

In a light picture frame use glue and drive nails both ways (FIG. 4-30C). Use corner clamps for holding and molding during nailing. The simplest clamp has screws that merely provide a grip. This arrangement is satisfactory, providing the joint is located closely. Another type of clamp has a screw that not only holds the parts but pushes them tightly together, usually with a roller arrangement against the rabbets.

A table saw with a fine-tooth blade will cut miters accurately if it has a suitable sliding guide (FIG. 4-30D). For many purposes there will be no

Fig. 4-30. Ways of ensuring accurate cutting and shaping.

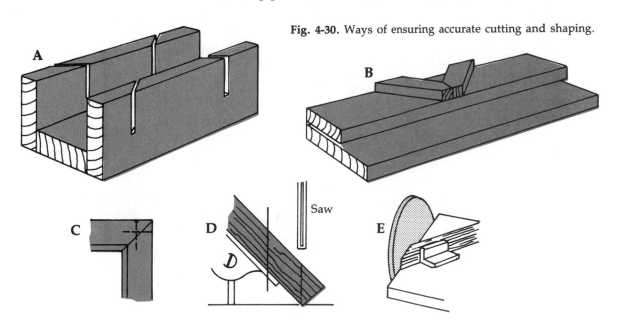

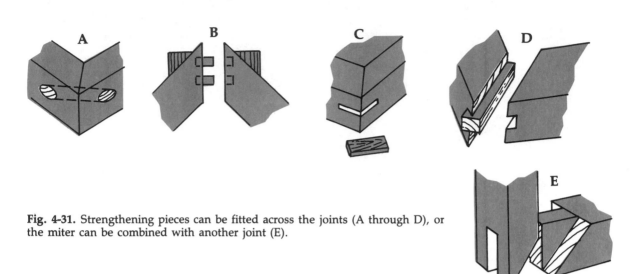

Fig. 4-31. Strengthening pieces can be fitted across the joints (A through D), or the miter can be combined with another joint (E).

need to plane or cut the meeting surfaces after this sawing. Another power tool that will true miters is a sanding disk, providing it is equipped with a table at right angles to its surface and a sliding guide that can be set to the angle required (FIG. 4-30E).

When the joint is larger or under more strain than can be resisted by glue and nails, there are other ways of constructing it. You can use dowels, arranged in the same way as nails, or placed diagonally across the joint and taken right through, if the exposed ends will not spoil the appearance (FIG. 4-31A).

You can also place stub dowels at right angles to the surfaces, but clamping this sort of joint brings a problem. One way of getting sufficient pressure is to glue or screw triangular blocks on to take a clamp (FIG. 4-31B). Then remove the blocks after the glue has set.

Pieces of veneer can be glued into saw cuts (FIG. 4-31C) or thicker pieces may form keys in grooves made in the meeting surfaces (FIG. 4-31D). In a load-bearing structure that would look better with a miter on the face, use a bridle joint with one face mitered (FIG. 4-31E).

Expansion Joints

As wood takes up and loses moisture, it expands and contracts, mostly in width. Most furniture is not exposes to greatly varying changes in heat and humidity, so properly seasoned wood can be expected to remain fairly stable. However, very wide boards expand or contract enough to affect joints or cause splitting if precautions are not taken. With modern plywood and other materials to use for wide surfaces, the problem is no longer acute, as these manufactured boards should maintain their size.

If you use solid wood for a panel, do not glue it into the grooved frame but allow it to be free to move. For a thicker panel, you can thin its edge which can serve as a decorative feature as well (FIG. 4-32A).

A solid wooden tabletop must be attached in a way that allows for movement. This can be done with buttons fixed to the top and having tongues to engage with grooves in the framework below (FIG. 4-32B) without glue. A groove may be plowed the full length to take several buttons, or notches can be cut for each button. If the top is made from a manufactured board, it can be fixed in the same way, although, since it remains a stable size, pocket screws can be used (FIG. 4-32C).

At one time, tongue and groove boards were used extensively in all kinds of construction as a means of covering large areas without gaps. Manufactured boards have taken over for most of these applications, but in furniture there are sometimes occasions when tongue and groove boards are still valuable. A tongue fitting into a groove (FIG. 4-33A) may be used to provide a better glue area than a simple butt joint. While this is good construction the main use of tongue and groove joints is in taking care of expansion and contraction. The area of the back of the cabinet, for instance, is covered by several boards about 6 inches wide. Their ends are nailed or screwed, but the joints between them are dry. To improve the appearance on the front, there may be chamfers, with a bend on one (FIG. 4-33B), so that widening or narrowing of the gap is not so obvious.

At one time there were special matched planes for making tongue and groove boards, but these are no longer available. The special plane cut both sides of the tongue at the same time, but the tongue can also be made by working two rabbets with a hand plane, table saw, or router.

A   **B**   **C**

Fig. 4-32. Expansion and contraction must be allowed for (A and B) with natural wood, but with manufactured board there may be direct screwing (C).

A Glued   **B** Front

Fig. 4-33. Before the days of wide panels of plywood and other manufactured board, narrow pieces had to be joined to make up a width. This may still be done for decorative effect, using a simple tongue and groove (A) or a joint with a bead on the front (B).

Lipping

Good quality cabinet wood has always been expensive, and for less noticeable parts, something of lesser quality can be used. Besides economy there are places where plywood or blockboard would actually be more appropriate than solid wood. In many places the substitute material has to be given an edge of the same wood as the main structure for the sake of appearance, however. This is referred to as *lipping*.

With solid wood it might be satisfactory to merely glue the lip on (FIG. 4-34A). With plywood or other manufactured board that present end grain to the joint, the lip might not be sufficiently secure. Using fine nails, which are punched below the surface and stopped, is not really a craftsmanlike way of giving extra security. It is better to use a tongue and groove joint (FIG. 4-34B). To secure an exact match, the lip may be made slightly wide and worked to size after the glue has set.

For a shelf or the bottom of a cabinet, a piece of comparatively thin plywood can be as strong as a piece of thicker solid wood that it replaces, but its edge has to be disguised. It can be glued and pinned in a rabbeted front piece (FIG. 4-34C).

If the plywood is thick enough, the joint will be improved if there is a tongue on the plywood mating with a groove in the lip (FIG. 4-34D). The ends of a shelf may have solid wood below the plywood to fit into a dado joint (FIG. 4-34E), and the rear edge may have a stiffening strip or may be supported on a ledge across the back of the cabinet.

There are occasions when, for the sake of appearance on both sides, thin plywood panels fit into a front piece lipped both ways (FIG. 4-34F). There will have to be some crosspieces between the panels as well, and a lengthwise strip at the back edge if this is exposed. In many constructions this can be avoided by using blockboard or similar material of suitable thickness.

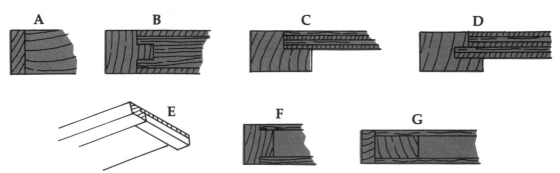

Fig. 4-34. Techniques for lipping or applying a stiff, attractive edge to plywood or other manufactured board.

If the built-up assembly consists of plywood over a frame and the plywood is unsupported for most of its area, there is a risk of distortion. The usual distortion is a concavity. In order to prevent this, you must face the other side as well. In a built-up door, for example, the inside should be faced with something of comparable type, although it need not have the high-quality surface of the front panel. In such a door the simplest construction is to take the plywood to the edges of the main framing and use a lip all around that matches the plywood (FIG. 4-34G).

Hinges

Correct hinging calls for care rather than a high degree of skill. If the hinge mounts on the surface, there is little trouble except to see that the door has enough clearance along its edge that it does not make contact and bind before it has fully shut.

Some hinges are decorative, but for many pieces of furniture, the hinge has to come in the joint. The basic hinge of this type is a *butt hinge*. If you examine such a hinge, you will notice that when the two flaps are closed to a parallel position there is a gap between them (FIG. 4-35A). This is to allow for a door or lid closing without the adjoining surfaces touching and stopping it.

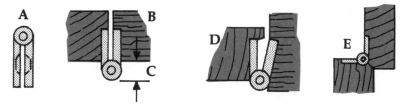

Fig. 4-35. Hinges have to be fitted so there is no ugly gap between the meeting surfaces while allowing the door or lid to swing clear.

In the best construction the two flaps are recessed into both surfaces (FIG. 4-35B). The knuckle has to stand clear of the surfaces, or the door will not swing far without binding on the door frame. How much clearance depends on the item being made. If the door will have to swing right back, the whole circle of the knuckle should be clear (FIG. 4-35C).

If the hinge is recessed entirely into the door, it will swing away with more clearance from the post. The center of the hinge knuckle should be level with the surface of the door or slightly away from it, even if the door does not have to swing right back. Recessing the hinge completely into the door so the other flap is only on the surface of the post is not good cabinetmaking practice, as all the weight of the door is taken by the screws in the post. It is all right to put the knuckle on the surface, but make a sloping cut into the post for the flap (FIG. 4-35D).

One of the few occasions when the knuckle of the hinge may come within the thickness of the wood is in a box lid which is to be stopped at a before-vertical position. The meeting edges are beveled and the hinges recessed far enough for the edges to meet and act as stops (FIG. 4-35E).

When you are marking for hinges, take care to see that the knuckles will all be in line, otherwise there will be distortion or strain, and movement of the screws. The length of a recess is best marked from the hinge itself. A gauge is set to the amount the flap is to be recessed in both directions (FIG. 4-36A). Marks across the grain should be cut in with a knife.

For small hinges it might be possible to cut deeply enough across the ends with a chisel. Otherwise use a fine saw diagonally, not only at the ends but at a few intermediate points to break up the waste. Use a chisel to follow the saw at the ends (FIG. 4-36B).

It is unwise to chop much with a chisel along the gauge lines, but you may make some light cuts on the waste side, then pare out the first bit of waste (FIG. 4-36C). In these shallow recesses it is very easy to go too deep. Try the hinge as cutting progresses. If a cut goes too far it may be possible to back out the hinge with veneer or paper.

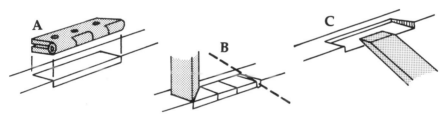

Fig. 4-36. Cutting the recess for a hinge is done by shallow saw cuts followed by chisel cuts.

In this case, you will have to make at least one trial assembly, before the door or lid moves satisfactorily. It is usually possible to put all the screws through the flap into the door, but then only use one screw in the other flap of each hinge for a trial movement. If all is well, drive in the other screws. Otherwise, withdraw a single screw and drive it through another hole in a corrected position, until the action is satisfactory. Then use a sliver of wood to plug any wrong hole before all screws are finally driven.

Hinges come with holes drilled and countersunk to take screws of a particular size. As it is important that screw heads should not foul each other and prevent the hinge closing, it is necessary to have screws of the right size and drive them squarely so they go flush into the countersinks. If screws of another size have to be used, prepare the holes in the hinges before doing other work.

5

Wood for Furniture

ALTHOUGH MANY MAN-MADE and other materials are now used in furniture, wood is still the first choice, particularly for structural parts. There is an attractiveness about wood that is lacking in most other materials. Apart from its appearance, it can be worked without great skill and without the need for elaborate equipment. Manufactured and natural forms of wood make up the bulk of materials used in making built-in furniture.

CHARACTERISTICS OF LUMBER

Wood varies in appearance, quality, and characteristics. These variations provide much of its attraction. They can be enhanced to provide interest and beauty.

As wood comes from trees, possible sizes depend on the original tree. Some trees grow tall and slender and so produce long, narrow boards. Others tend to have thick trunks of no great height, so that boards may be of considerable widths but no great length. Most furniture-making woods are available in all the sizes you are likely to need, but it sometimes happens that suitable sizes are unavailable in a particular choice of wood.

In any tree a part of the wood is *heartwood*, and around it there is *sapwood* (FIG. 5-1A). As the tree grows, more layers form on the outside, and some

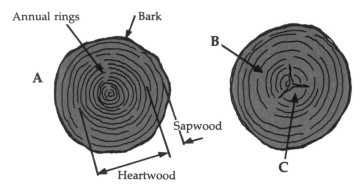

Fig. 5-1. The middle of a tree produces heartwood (A) the most durable wood, but there may be flaws: cup or ring shakes (B) and heart or star shakes (C).

of the inner sapwood changes into heartwood. The annual rings form the grain marking.

In some woods there is a pronounced difference in appearance between sapwood and heartwood. In other woods it is difficult to distinguish them. In general, heartwood is much more durable than sapwood, but there are some woods in which there is little difference in durability. Where possible, all wood used for furniture should be heartwood.

As a tree grows, *shakes* may develop. These are cracks that go around the grain as cup or ring shakes (FIG. 5-1B) or across the grain as heart or star shakes (FIG. 5-1C). These do not affect the quality of the wood, but furniture wood has to be cut around them. When a tree has been felled, it has to be seasoned to dry out the sap to a controlled small amount. Cracks might develop during drying, particularly at the ends. These do not affect quality or other characteristics, but they will have to be allowed for and cut around when preparing furniture parts.

Wood will always absorb and give up moisture with changes in humidity. This affects the stability of the wood. There is little effect along the grain, but a board may expand in its width as it takes up moisture and shrink as it loses moisture. It will also warp, and the risk of warping and its probable direction is related to the way the board is cut from the tree.

CONVERSION OF LOGS TO LUMBER

If boards are cut straight across the log, a board with the grain marks across the thickness is unlikely to warp at all (FIG. 5-2A); but boards nearer the circumference will tend to become hollow (FIG. 5-2B). If the end of a board is examined, the board's relation to the whole section of tree can be visualized and the risk of warping estimated. A convenient way to remember what might happen is to think of the curved grain rings as trying to straighten themselves out (FIG. 5-2C). If the wood is in a round

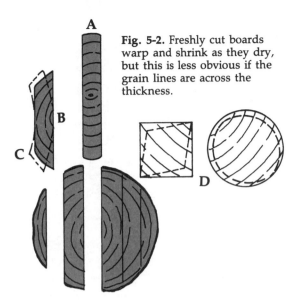

Fig. 5-2. Freshly cut boards warp and shrink as they dry, but this is less obvious if the grain lines are across the thickness.

or square section, distortion is likely to be a shrinking in the direction of the grain (FIG. 5-2D) as the wood dries.

Sometimes wood is cut to give the best grain appearance. To get the maximum number of boards with attractive markings, they are cut from the outside inwards (FIG. 5-3A). Besides grain there are *medullary rays*, which radiate from the center outwards. In many woods they are invisible, but in some woods they are sufficiently prominent to provide a decorative effect if the wood is cut along their lines. This is particularly so in some types of oak. A radially cut board is then described as *quarter sawn, figured oak, wainscot oak,* or *silver grain* (FIG. 5-3B).

Cutting many boards exactly radially results in much waste so it is common to make the cuts in layers (FIG. 5-3C) so that all but the outermost boards can be expected to show markings from the medullary rays. Wood

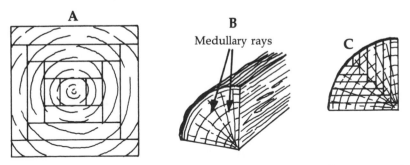

Fig. 5-3. Wood may be cut to get the best appearance of grain (A), or to use the figuring of rays in oak and some other woods (B and C).

cut this way will be more expensive, but in suitable types the effect is very attractive.

LUMBER SIZES AND GRADES

Much furniture-grade wood is sold in nonstandard sizes or prepared to suit the customer. The owner of a shop with suitable equipment will find it most economical to buy wood in stock sections and cut it down to suit his needs. Even then, if stock sections from the local yard can be used, there will be a saving in cost and effort. Standard sizes are most applicable to lumber used for house construction and similar work, but may be found with the higher quality woods needed for furniture.

Grades

Lumber is available in two grades: *select* and *common*. Select is subdivided into A, B, C, and D in decreasing quality. Common lumber starts where select leaves off and is graded 1, 2, 3, and 4 in descending quality. The main difference between select and common lumber is in the wood's ability to take a finish where the grain would show through.

Grades A and B obviously are just about free of blemishes or defects in the grain, but these may be more obvious in grades C and D. Common grades are suitable for use where they do not have to take a finish or where appearance is unimportant. Grades 1 and 2 have uses in internal work in furniture, but grades 3 and 4 may have too many defects—such as large knots, knotholes, or confused, rough grain—to be used in furniture.

It is possible that a board with a low grade because of a defect in one place may yield wood of adequate quality in another part. For economy the buyer might not want to buy wood of a higher grade than necessary. If you have an opportunity to look over the stock in a lumberyard, it is often possible to find economical pieces you can use by cutting around defects yourself.

Sizes

Lumber is sized as it is sawn. Machine planing takes off at least 1/8 inch. This means that a piece of lumber described as 2 × 4 inches which has been machine planed all round will actually be about 1¾ × 3¾ inches. The term *board* is applied to wood for sale that is over 8 inches wide and less than 2 inches thick.

Smaller pieces are called *strips*. Larger sections are referred to as *timbers*, although in some places *timber* is a word used as an alternative to *lumber*.

Lumberyards that do not cut the wood to size on the premises might keep stock lengths in multiples of 2 feet, from 6 feet upward. Purchases should be arranged to allow for this. Charges may be according to length and section, but it is best to know what is meant by *board foot* in case that is the method of quoting prices. This reduces the size to the equivalent of a square foot, 1 inch thick. Hence a piece of wood 1 foot square and 1 inch thick is one board foot. So is a piece 2 inches wide and 6 feet long × 1 inch thick. A thicker piece has to be reduced to 1 inch by increasing the surface area, so a piece of wood 2 inches thick need only be half a square foot on the surface to represent one board foot.

There is an advantage in buying in quantity rather than just getting wood for the project at hand. You will find that certain stock sections are particularly useful in many pieces of built-in furniture, and it is economical to build up a store so you can take wood from the shelf or rack as needed. It would be unwise to buy unusual material that might never be needed again, but even then, much of the joy of amateur craftsmanship is in designing furniture around available material.

Because of difficulty in obtaining long or wide pieces in some woods (caused by the sizes of trees), extra wide or long pieces may cost proportionately more than smaller pieces. It is always best to visit a lumberyard armed with your detailed cutting list; then wood from stock can be found to suit items economically. This is much better than totaling all the pieces of a certain section and asking for one long piece, which may carry a premium because of its length.

Similar arguments apply to widths. It is usually most economical to accept the narrowest pieces that will suit your purpose rather than to ask for wider boards to cut down. However, there are exceptions. Very narrow pieces might be cut from the waste from cutting large boards and might be sapwood. Narrow strips might be cut from branches. A wide board has to be cut from the trunk of the tree and should be all heartwood. The best wood is more likely to be in the wide piece, and if this is what you want, buy a wide board and cut it down, even if it costs more than the equivalent narrow pieces.

WOOD TYPES

Wood is very broadly divided into hardwoods and softwoods. Although most hardwoods are harder than most softwoods, the names are not really very apt. Hardwoods are those trees that have broad leaves, nearly all of which are lost during the winter. Softwoods are trees with needle leaves, which are mostly retained during the winter. The average woodworker will mostly handle softwoods from pines, firs, spruces and the like. All the better woods that are used for furniture, particularly where a polished finish is used, are hardwoods.

It is difficult to keep track of all the kinds of wood. Although certain woods are acceptable for particular purposes and are in fairly regular supply, there are many others that are equally suitable for the same purposes. There are upwards of 3000 separate species of trees with commercial value, so any advice on woods can only be regarded as a guide.

Quite often a piece of built-in furniture will have to match some existing furniture, and that will determine what wood to use, at least for the visible parts. Sometimes, however, contrasting wood can be quite effective. A room with dark furniture might benefit from something with light facing, or vice versa.

The use of the furniture should also be considered. Something in a child's room might get rougher treatment than a similar item elsewhere, so the wood should be one that will take knocks without showing them much and should certainly not be likely to splinter. A corner cupboard might not be at much risk from knocks because of its position, so a softer wood could be sufficiently durable.

Some of the more choice woods are very expensive. They might still be worth having, but it is sometimes possible to use a cheaper wood with a sufficiently similar grain marking, then finish it with stain and polish to produce an effective piece of furniture at a much lower price. Of course, if the final finish is to be paint, it is more important to have wood that will finish smoothly, with no pronounced grain.

Softwoods

Although softwoods grow in many parts of the world, those used by woodworkers are mostly from the northern temperate zones of America, Europe, and Asia. Unfortunately, common names are not always the same, and the same wood may have a different name if it comes from a different place. Some are listed below with their alternate names.

Cedar, Western Red. Soft, reddish-brown, straight grained, and available in long lengths.

Cypress. Grows in swamps. Has a greasy feel and a sour smell. Straight-grained, light brown. Will withstand heat and moisture. Does not take glue very well.

Columbian Pine, Douglas Pine, Oregon Pine, Douglas Fir. One of the harder softwoods, straight-grained, reddish-brown. Raised grain and resin make the wood unsuitable for face work, but it may be used structurally in furniture.

Hemlock. Does not take a fine finish and is more of an external wood than one for furniture.

Larch. Medium texture, easily worked, light orange-brown color.

Pine, Parana. Brazilian wood, pale straw color, and available in wide boards.

Pine, Pitch. Heavy because of considerable resin. Has pronounced grain. Difficult to bring to a good finish.

Other Pines. Eastern white pine and ponderosa pine are light, with little strength. Sugar pine grows into large trees; it will finish smoothly despite large knots, which may be used as a decorative feature. Western white pine is similar. None of these is very durable if exposed.

Redwood, Yellow Deal, Red Deal, Red Pine, Scots Pine, Northern Pine. Reddish-brown, straight-grained, some resin. Suitable for internal construction.

Sequoia, California Redwood. Very large trees, so great lengths and widths obtainable. Rather open and porous, reddish-brown, and straight grained. Not very strong.

Spruce, Sitka, Silver Spruce. A combination of lightness with a strong, straight grain makes this a choice for aircraft construction and yacht spars. Not a furniture choice unless easily obtained.

Spruce, Whitewood, White Deal. Sometimes considered a poorer quality redwood. Near white, with some knots and resin pockets.

Hardwoods

Although a great variety of hardwoods are native to North America, many others are imported because of their special qualities. Distribution varies according to geography and climate. When making traditional furniture, the indigenous wood of the region is often chosen. Some of the woods indigenous to various regions are listed below, but these lists are not exhaustive, and some trees spread over into other regions.

Northern Region. Ash, aspen, basswood, yellow birch, butternut, cherry, elm, hickory, locust, hard maple, oak, walnut.

Central Region. White ash, basswood, beech, buckeye, chestnut, cottonwood, American elm, hackberry, shagbark hickory, locust, hard maple, white oak, sycamore, yellow poplar, walnut.

Appalachian Region. Ash, beech, red oak, white oak, hard maple.

Southern Region. Ash, basswood, beech, birch, cottonwood, elm, hackberry, hickory, locust, maple, red and cherry-bark oak, pecan, sweet and red gum, sycamore, black willow.

There are some very hard woods, such as greenheart, which will sink in water; but these do not have furniture uses. The softest and lightest of what are technically hardwoods is balsa—which is softer and lighter than most softwoods. It has no normal furniture application.

The woods listed below are hardwood examples, which may provide comparisons when other woods are being considered.

Ash. Straight, rather coarse grain. Valued for its springiness and bending qualities.

Basswood, Lime. Light, close-grained; easy to work and suitable for carving.

Beech, Red or White. Tough, close grain. Used for tools. Very good for turning on lathe.

Chestnut. Looks and works like oak, but has no figuring when quarter-sawn.

Elm. Durable, with confused grain that resists splitting. Not of much use in furniture except traditional designs.

Gaboon. Nondurable African wood that looks like mahogany. Used for lightweight plywood.

Red Gum, Sweet Gum, Satin Walnut. Soft, even brown color with little sign of grain. Stains well. Twists and warps if not built into other parts.

Maple. Varies from light yellow to brown.

Mahogany, Spanish and Cuban. Rich brown with close grain. Original furniture mahogany, but there are many more.

Mahogany, Honduras; Baywoods. Lightweight with light brown color. A furniture wood.

Mahogany, African. There are several of these, and not all true mahoganies; but some are suitable for furniture.

Red Oak. The usual open-grained brown oak, with a pink shade present. Has figuring in quarter-sawn boards. Large boards obtainable.

Oak, English. The oak used for medieval ships and furniture. Brown, open-grained, with prominent figuring when quarter-sawn. Very strong and durable.

Oak, Japanese and Austrian. More mellow and easier to work than English oak. Good furniture woods.

Poplar, yellow; Canary Wood; American Whitewood. Even, close-grained, yellow wood. Varying quality, but usually easy to work. Similar to basswood and sometimes confused with it.

Sapele. Looks like mahogany. Its attractive grain may be difficult to work. Used for making plywood.

Sycamore. Whitish-yellow, close-grained wood with sometimes a figure or ripple marking visible in the grain. Good for turning on lathe. Its near white color makes it suitable for use with food.

Teak. This is a dark brown wood that bleaches to near white in the sun. It may be difficult to work because of its resin. It is very durable even when not treated in any way. Not usual for furniture.

Walnut, American Black Walnut. A shade of purple mixed with dark brown. Takes a good finish.

MANUFACTURED WOOD

All wood is prepared for use by being cut from logs and seasoned. This may be considered a manufacturing process, but there are a number of wood forms, particularly in panels, in which manufacturing is taken further. These have revolutionized furniture making and made the construction of broad surfaces and panels much easier, with results superior to anything achieved with solid wood. The use of plywood or other manufactured wood panels is good, modern cabinetmaking practice. The only places where these things would not be appropriate would be in reproduction work or the repair of antiques.

Plywood

In its early days plywood was often rough and insecurely bonded by the less satisfactory glues then available. Modern plywood is extremely strong and stable, and finishes to match anything on solid wood are possible.

Plywood Veneers. Plywood is made from *veneers*, which are thin slices of wood. Most veneers for plywood are rotary-cut, with a knife slicing off the correct thickness in a long length from a rotating log (FIG. 5-4A). The grain marking will not be the same as that from wood cut across by sawing. As the log rotates, similar grain markings will be repeated at each complete turn. If you examine a plywood panel you can see a repeat of the grain pattern across the panel. The distance between these repeats is the same as the circumference at the time of the cut.

With veneers cut this way the grain marking will not be a match with any solid wood from the same species of tree. This usually does not matter, as the color should match and the grain appearance can be quite attractive.

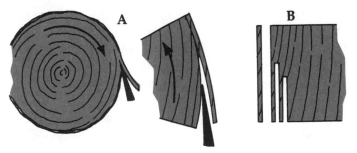

Fig. 5-4. Veneers may be cut continuously around a log (A) by slicing (B) or sawing (C).

Veneers of some wood are sliced with a knife across the wood as in (FIG. 5-4B), or they may be cut with a saw as in (FIG. 5-4C). In both cases the width is limited by the thickness of the original piece of wood. Such veneers are not usually made into plywood, but they can be used to face it. They have the same grain markings as solid wood from the same tree.

The thickness of veneers made into plywood varies. Some aircraft plywood has three layers within a total thickness of 1/25 inch, or 1 mm. In furniture plywood a veneer thickness about 1½ mm is common, but veneer thickness has to be regulated according to the total thickness required. Much early plywood had three veneers, hence the name 3-ply. Many other numbers of veneers are used, but 3-ply is common for thinner sheets. The three plies may be the same thickness (FIG. 5-5A), or the center one may be thicker (FIG. 5-5B) to give a more balanced strength. Whatever the number of veneers, the outer ones are normally in the same direction (FIG. 5-5C).

A

B

C

Fig. 5-5. Plywood may have three plies of equal thickness (A), or the center ply may be thicker (B). Outer grains are usually aligned (C). A compensating veneer opposite the face side (D) reduces warpage.

D

Glue in plywood is normally a synthetic type, usually with a good resistance to dampness, so the plywood remains flat and does not expand and contract to any extent that will matter.

Many woods are used for making plywood, but there are some which are unsuitable for rotary cutting of veneers or are not obtainable in suitable sizes. Some woods only show the beauty of their grain if crosscut; rotary cutting, even if the wood permitted this, would not result in as attractive an appearance. Some woods are rare and expensive, so their use in solid form would be wasteful. Many of these can be cut into veneers so that their beauty can be spread as far as possible. The veneers are then put on a cheaper base material.

Plywood is ideal for this, and panels may be bought already faced with veneers of rare woods, either as an overall arrangement of strips butted together side by side, or with veneer pieces arranged in a pattern. Normally the face veneers are thinner than those that go to make up the plywood, and it is usual to put a compensating veneer (not necessarily of choice wood) on the opposite side (FIG. 5-5D). This balances stresses in the plywood and resists any tendency to warping.

Sizes and Grades. Plywood is made in panels of many sizes. A common width is 4 feet and most panels are 8 feet long; but longer panels are made. Thicknesses start at 3/16 inch or less and go up to about 3/4 inch. Some manufacturers use metric thicknesses, from 4 to 18 mm.

The number of plies in a thickness varies. A larger number should result in a stiffer panel for the same thickness: 5-ply wood that is 1/4 of an inch thick should be stiffer than 3-ply wood that is 1/4 of an inch thick.

Most plywood manufacturers divide their products into interior and exterior grades, with the latter able to withstand outdoor weather. A marine grade is superior to the exterior grade and suitable for use in boats. Within each grade there may be many variations of veneer. A cabinet-quality veneer is without flaws; this may be on one or both outer surfaces, depending on the intended use. A less important surface may have flaws such as knots (or knots might have been cut out and plugged), and there may be small splits in the veneers.

The grade of veneer in the core may vary. For greatest strength and for some exterior applications, it is important to have good-quality veneers inside. Elsewhere inferior veneers may be used inside without affecting the use of the plywood. Edge joints between internal veneers should meet for greatest strength, but for some purposes slight gaps will not matter. Where plywood for these lesser qualities can be used, the price should be less.

Blockboard and Chipboards

Thick plywood is expensive, so alternatives are used, most often with a core made of solid wood strips, collectively called *blockboard*. Like plywood, blockboard has outer veneers, but the center is made up of solid strips, with the pieces glued to each other and to the veneers. The grain of the inner pieces crosses that of the veneers, which are often thicker than the outer plies of plywood.

Blockboard with narrow strips inside is often called *laminboard* (FIG. 5-6A). If wider pieces are used, it is *battenboard* (FIG. 5-6B). In some forms the outer veneers are a double thickness, which gives an increased resistance to any tendency to twist or warp.

A thicker board made up from wood particles embedded in synthetic resin is called *particleboard* or *chipboard* (FIG. 5-6C). This is unattractive and so has to be covered when used in exposed places.

Chipboard may be veneered during manufacture, either with wood veneer or plastic with a wood grain appearance. These boards, in many stock sizes, may be veneered on edges and ends as well as the surfaces (FIG. 5-6D) and sold under various trade names. If a design can be adapted to utilize a stock size of board, this material will make attractive worktops,

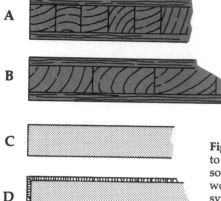

Fig. 5-6. There are alternatives to the thicker plywood, with solid wood cores (A and B) or wood particles mixed with synthetic resin (C and D).

shelves, and room dividers. If a veneered board has to be cut and the cut edge will be exposed, it has to be veneered by hand.

Matching veneers are available from some makers. These may be self-adhesive, or they might have to be fixed with a contact adhesive. As the base material is a plastic resin rather than wood, many ordinary wood glues do not work.

You might have problems using screws or other fasteners with chipboard, but special attachments and plugs can be glued in to take screws.

Hardboard

Wood pulp may be manufactured into boards. There are many grades, mainly dependent on the density of the boards. Loosely bonded boards are used for insulation, and others are more like card than wood; but quite a hard material can be made when a suitable bonding agent is used along with sufficient compression. For furniture construction this hardboard has some uses for cheap backs of cabinets or drawer bottoms. *Masonite* is one well-known make.

Hardboard is commonly available in sheet sizes similar to those of plywood: ⅛ inch is the usual thickness, although others are available. In the basic sheet there is one hard, smooth surface, and the other is rough and patterned. It is possible to get sheets smooth on both sides, as well as panels with fluted and other patterned effects.

Providing the original surface is not broken through by tools or sanding, hardboard can be extremely durable in the better grades. The softer and cheaper qualities are not really suitable for permanent furniture.

Some of the better boards are treated with oil or some other means during manufacture that gives them a tougher, water-resistant quality.

They are sometimes described as *oil-tempered*. Although these are intended mainly for exposed surfaces, they are the best choice for furniture. Hardboard takes most of the finishes used on ordinary wood, and the smooth surface without blemishes makes a good base for paint.

Prepared Strips

Besides wood in rectangular sections, many other stock sections are obtainable, and some of these can be used in built-in furniture. A visit to a lumberyard or a supplier specializing in woodwork supplies will acquaint you with what is available.

There are, for example, round sections. In the smaller sizes these are described as dowel rods, and they are in suitable hardwoods for use in making dowel joints; but as the lengths are often 3 feet or more, it is possible to use them as rails or posts in some constructions. Larger sections work for broom handles, but they have additional uses such as a rail to take clothes hangers.

Many standard molding sections are available as well. Some of these are designed to cover plywood edges or give a finish to corner-lapped joints. In some constructions the use of moldings allows simpler joints between parts, as they can be covered. Anyone proud of his or her woodworking skill will want to make his or her furniture by acceptable methods, but restrained use of manufactured moldings will often enhance the result.

The larger moldings are made of white pine or other softwood, so they require a painted finish. But there are hardwood moldings usable for cabinetwork, such as picture frame moldings.

Decorative pieces of wood can be bought to glue onto furniture. These may be embossed to look like carving. The fastidious cabinetmaker is likely to feel that they are inferior substitutes for the real thing and avoid them.

USING MANUFACTURED BOARDS

Although most furniture can be made from natural wood—and this is preferable when there is a traditional theme to be maintained—much use can be made of manufactured boards in various forms. Some information on the use of these boards has been given in earlier chapters, and some of the techniques are the same as for solid wood; but since many of the projects in the following chapters can be made with manufactured boards, a summary of special considerations and methods is appropriate here.

Surfaces

Most boards are supplied already surfaced with veneer or a plastic laminate. This is on both broad surfaces and the long edges, but not always at the ends. Unless the base material is very thick and can resist warping from the pull on one side, it is best to have the material veneered on both sides. For economy the veneer on the second side can be of a plain type for locations where the second side is hidden.

Base Material

How the board is worked depends mainly on the base material. If it is built up, whether with many laminations of veneer or with a solid core, it can be treated in nearly the same way as solid wood.

The material is more likely to be a particleboard in which wood chips and resin are bonded together. Working this material depends to a certain extent on the consistency and proportions. In many cases the amount of wood in the mixture is sufficient for the whole to have characteristics fairly close to those of solid wood. In other cases the mixture may have more tendency to crumble and chip if not worked correctly. If manufactured board of a type you have not previously used has to be cut and a new edge finished, it is best to treat it as this more brittle type at first.

Sizes

One of the advantages of manufactured boards is the availability of stock sizes. But to take advantage of this, you must design the furniture accordingly. Available sizes must be checked and allowed for early in the planning stage. This has a limiting effect on possible designs, and there is an inevitable slab appearance about many furniture items made from manufactured board. This plainness can be broken up by the use of molding, turned parts, and shaped pieces made from solid wood.

Some veneered boards can be matched with solid-wood parts, but boards covered with plastic are not so easily matched, and these are better used with painted parts. Or the plastic-surfaced panel may be separated from the wood parts by a molding or contrasting strip.

Cutting

Care in cutting is needed in order to prevent the veneer from splintering or breaking away. Always cut through the veneer all around with a knife before sawing (FIG. 5-7A), whether using a handsaw or power saw. A fine saw is particularly important with a resin-rich particleboard.

An ordinary steel saw will do, but if much sawing of manufactured board is necessary, use a saw with specially tipped teeth that resist blunting.

Crumbling or chipping of an edge is less likely if you handsaw cuts at a fairly flat angle (B) or a circular saw just goes through. Toward the end of a cut, make sure the waste, as well as the main part of the board, is supported, and take the final strokes slowly.

Edging

Plane the edges, if possible, preferably by hand with a tool that has a low cutting angle. If you use power planing, pass the material over the cutters slowly; faster progress might cause breaking out. Power sanding is less satisfactory, as this tends to round edges. As a cut edge might have to butt against another piece or be veneered, the surface must be truly flat right to the edges.

The most convenient way to veneer an edge is to use a self-adhesive strip. This ensures that the glue will suit the material. If you use a plain veneer, it might be necessary to experiment to find a suitable glue if there are no recommendations with the board or veneer. An impact adhesive is usually satisfactory.

To obtain a good adhesion right to the edge, it is best to have the edge veneer oversize (FIG. 5-8A) so it can be trimmed afterwards. To minimize the risk of an exposed edge lifting, there should be a very slight bevel—perhaps just one stroke of a finely set plane (FIG. 5-8B).

A plastic surface can be cut and treated in a very similar way, but special scrapers will trim an edge better than a plane. A fine file can be used on a beveled edge.

Manufactured boards may appear flimsy when used over much length, even if they actually have sufficient stiffness. You can obtain a more

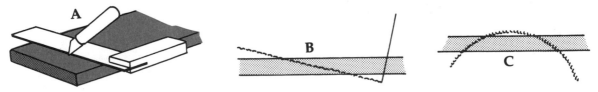

Fig. 5-7. Particle and other manufactured board can be cut with woodworking tools.

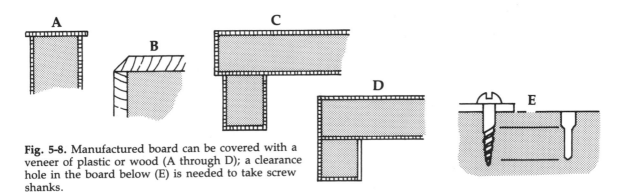

Fig. 5-8. Manufactured board can be covered with a veneer of plastic or wood (A through D); a clearance hole in the board below (E) is needed to take screw shanks.

substantial appearance by using a strip of the same material set back a little below an edge (FIG. 5-8C), or thickening an edge so a new veneer or strip of Formica can be put on (FIG. 5-8D). This can be anything from a doubling of the thickness to quite a deep apron on a bar front or similar place.

Reasonable success can be expected from driving ordinary wood screws into manufactured board, but with a particle board, drill sizes should be carefully chosen. Otherwise a screw might shear off before it is fully driven, or there may be breaking out at the surface, or even complete bursting of the board.

With most boards a hole should go the full depth of the screw, and if any part of the unthreaded neck will enter the board, there should be a clearance hole to take it (FIG. 5-8E). In some cases it might be more satisfactory to use a self-tapping screw.

Fastening Manufactured Boards

In some manufactured boards, direct screwing might be satisfactory for attaching fittings or for places where there is only a light load; but at points of greater stress, something else may be preferable. In places where the other side is hidden, a bolt can go right through to a washer and nut.

Dowels make satisfactory joints in most manufactured boards. The dowel diameter should not be much more than one-third the total thickness of a board. In a simple T-joint, use at least three dowels and arrange them about 2 inches apart, with the outer dowels not less than about ¾ inch from the edges to reduce the risk of damage when drilling. Have the work and drill supported in relation to each other to reduce any risk of breaking out.

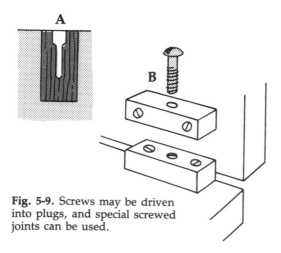

Fig. 5-9. Screws may be driven into plugs, and special screwed joints can be used.

To strengthen a screwed joint, use a plug in a hole. This can be a piece of dowel glued in (FIG. 5-9A), but it is better to use a plastic insert designed for the purpose. Even when the base material is plywood or blockboard, an insert will make a stronger joint in edge screwing, where the threads would otherwise only come on loose-gripping end grain.

There are plastic joint pieces that can be used in right-angled corners. Two or more should be used, depending on the total width. These are particularly practical if the parts will be dismantled at some time. In one type, two plastic blocks screw to the panels and are joined by a screw (FIG. 5-9B).

Drawers

Joints have to be kept simple. It is possible to groove most manufactured boards to take a lip of solid wood, but dovetail and mortise and tenon joints are not likely to be successful. This affects drawer construction. Corners can overlap and be glued and screwed, and a false overlapping front used (FIG. 5-10A). The plywood or hardboard bottom also overlaps instead of being slotted in. This means it is better to use slides at the sides (FIG. 5-10B) instead of runners underneath.

It is usually better for drawer construction to be in solid wood. One way of using veneered board for drawer fronts is to make them sloping so the lower edge of a front hides the drawer runners. This provides a lip which can be used for a handle (FIG. 5-10C).

Veneered boards are supplied with true surfaces already sanded. The veneer is quite thin. This means there is little room for heavy sanding, and it is important that the existing surface is not damaged. Vise jaws should be covered with some material which is smooth and no harder than the veneer, perhaps paper or cloth. This is also advisable on the bench top. Plastic-surfaced boards are less susceptible to damage, but if

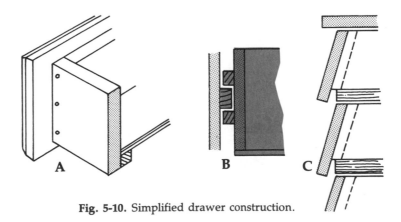

Fig. 5-10. Simplified drawer construction.

any damage is done, it cannot be repaired. Handle these boards in the same cautious way as veneered boards.

The adhesives used to fix veneers and laminated-plastic surfaces to the core material in manufactured boards are usually highly water-resistant. Some might weaken if exposed to exceptionally moist conditions. Excessive moisture might also affect some core materials. Where a board is veneered all around, it is unlikely that moisture will penetrate enough to have any effect on the core or adhesive except in complete immersion.

When a board has been cut and the edge is exposed, some protection against moisture should be provided. On a cut end that will be joined with dowels to another piece, glue in the joint might be all that is needed to keep out moisture. On an exposed edge, painting or varnishing will probably prevent penetration of moisture. It might be better to first give the edge a coating of waterproof glue, applied like paint, and then sand lightly before painting.

Other liquids may be expected to have the same effect on veneers as they would on solid wood, so the appropriate surface treatment should be used. The plastic used for most laminated surfaces is unaffected by most common liquids, so these surfaces are appropriate for places where food is to be prepared or drinks served.

6

Upholstery

NOT MANY BUILT-IN PIECES OF FURNITURE require upholstery, but such things as window seats and seats built into recesses might be better finished with something more than a wooden base and back. It might be possible to make the seat sufficiently comfortable with loose cushions, but with modern materials it is not difficult to provide something comparable with the padding and covering of an ordinary chair.

Traditional materials have been largely superseded by synthetic ones. The only snag with man-made materials is that they do not "breath." Consequently, prolonged use may cause dampness to accumulate under them. If a built-in seat is to have a piece of plywood or solid wood under upholstery or cushioning of synthetic material, it is best to perforate the wood. A piece of perforated hardboard could be used, but it is probably better to use somewhat larger holes in plywood (FIG. 6-1).

A matte surface seems to attract less moisture than a glossy one. If the cushions are loose, they are less likely to slip on a matte surface.

If there is to be no resilience in the support, any cushioning needs to be at least 3 inches thick for a seat, 4 inches or more for greater comfort or sleeping. The alternative is to use a flexible support under thinner cushioning, usually in the form of webbing.

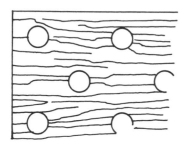

Fig. 6-1. The wood under a cushion of synthetic material in a built-in seat should be perforated.

WEBBING

The webbing may be fabric type with strips 1½ inch or wider and with only minimal stretch, or a rubberized type that possesses some elasticity. The first is traditional, but use the other if you want the seat to conform more to body shape.

Whichever type you use, you should interweave it on a wooden frame of sufficient stiffness (FIG. 6-2). The closeness of weave depends on the strength required and the density of what goes above. A rather loosely made cushion would require a relatively close weave of webbing.

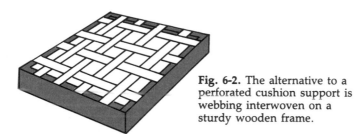

Fig. 6-2. The alternative to a perforated cushion support is webbing interwoven on a sturdy wooden frame.

It is difficult to get sufficient tension by hand and to control the strain while fastening the webbing, so a strainer should be made or bought (FIG. 6-3A). Sizes are suggested in the accompanying illustration, but you can adapt these to suit available material. The webbing is looped around a rod to hold it for tightening. The rod can be a piece of doweling, or almost any scrap piece of wood, not necessarily round.

Webbing is usually fastened with tacks or large-head nails. At one side a little surplus webbing is allowed to extend, then three tacks are driven (FIG. 6-3B). The surplus piece is turned over, and three more tacks are driven. With a woven webbing, the end should be turned under to prevent fraying (FIG. 6-3C).

The strainer should have a beveled or rounded end. Place this against the frame at the opposite side, dip the webbing through the slot, and insert the peg. Then grip the excess webbing by hand (FIG. 6-3D). Levering downward, pull the webbing taut and drive in the first three tacks. It

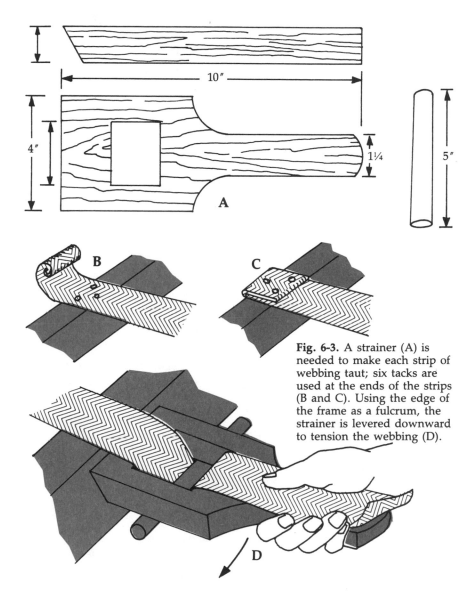

Fig. 6-3. A strainer (A) is needed to make each strip of webbing taut; six tacks are used at the ends of the strips (B and C). Using the edge of the frame as a fulcrum, the strainer is levered downward to tension the webbing (D).

is important to keep about the same tension on each length of webbing, otherwise the seat might settle unevenly after prolonged use.

PADDING

Various forms of foam rubber and plastic are available, either in pieces to cut to size or in cushion shapes. With some forms of built-in seats or beds, it is best at the planning stage to check on the available sizes of upholstery padding and arrange the other work accordingly. An advantage of using a stock size is that the ends as well as the surface will be in a smooth-finished form, usually with rounded corners. However, if the best rounded edge you can achieve with knife or scissors is not as uniform as you wish, the covering material can probably coax it into an acceptable curve.

Where furniture has inaccessible parts, as most built-in furniture will, it is usually best to arrange the upholstered parts to lift out. If cushions are store-bought, they can be merely placed in position; but you are more likely to have to make up something to fit the available space.

CUSHIONS AND BASES

Making cushions is outside the scope of this book, but a few hints about cushions are in order. It is best to cover the rubber or plastic lining with one or more layers of cloth, then make a removable cover from material that matches the other furniture. Then arrange the buttons or other fasteners along what will be the rear edge. The cushion need not be a rounded form, but a block of foam with squared edges and slightly rounded angles can be covered so it is a close fit into the available space. A long seat will be covered better with several sections of cushion rather than with one long one.

If a rigid base for the upholstery is desired, the base can be plywood and designed to lift out. A box seat in a recess may have a lip at the front so that the complete upholstered top is located but can be removed to give access to the interior (FIG. 6-4A). Depending on size, the base may be thin plywood with a frame (FIG. 6-4B), or for more rigidity it could be thicker plywood or blockboard, with or without framing (FIG. 6-4C).

COVERING THE FURNITURE

The buttons on upholstery often are not just decorative. They prevent the covering and filling from moving in relation to each other. This is essential for anything except the smallest assembly.

With framed plywood locate the foam on the base, then fit the lining cloth over it and turn the cloth under. Fix it with tacks around the edge at 3-inch intervals. Use only enough tension to bring the cloth into close contact with the foam (FIG. 6-4D).

If the cloth edge will not be covered, turn under the cut edge to prevent fraying. If the underside is to be covered, put the covering on and bring it up around the sides (FIG. 6-4E). If you intend to use for storing blankets or bedding, a cloth lining for the lid is preferable.

The ease of fitting the outer covering material depends on its type. A loosely woven fabric is amenable to pulling into shape, but imitation leather, which is a plastic coating on a fabric backing has little stretch and requires careful manipulation. It might be necessary to do some work over.

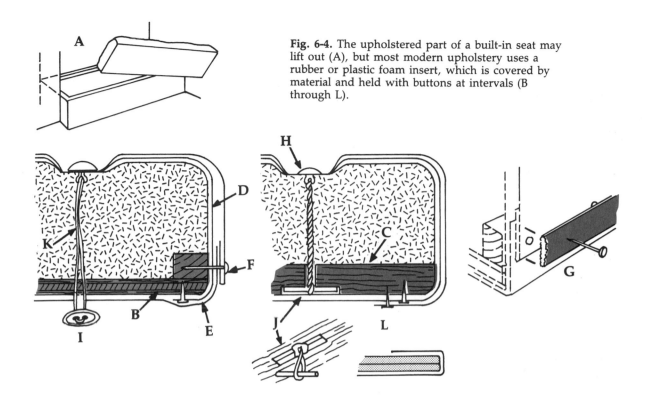

Fig. 6-4. The upholstered part of a built-in seat may lift out (A), but most modern upholstery uses a rubber or plastic foam insert, which is covered by material and held with buttons at intervals (B through L).

Stretch the covering material over the area to be covered and tack along opposite sides first, then do the other sides, pleating the corners neatly. You may fix the material with roundhead or decorative upholstery nails (FIG. 4-4F). Or you may use a row of plain tacks and cover these with a strip of gimp (trimming) braid (FIG. 4-4G).

Holes for the thread and buttons are probably best drilled in the wood base before assembly. The holes are usually arranged so a pattern is formed. Their spacing depends on the materials used. The stiffer coverings do not need as many as the more flexible materials, but more may be used for the sake of appearance.

You might want to use upholstery buttons that can be covered with the same material as the covering. Alternatively, any button with a loop on the back can be used on the surface (FIG. 6-4H) and underneath, an ordinary 2-hole coat button can be used (FIG. 6-4I).

If you want a flush finish allow a wooden or wire pin to spring into a slot (FIG. 6-4J), where it is hidden by the cloth lining. Use a stout thread, as breakages in use could be a nuisance. Carpet and sailmaking thread work well. Most synthetic threads are stronger size for size than natural fiber threads and will not rot.

Special long upholsterer's needles are available, some of them pointed at both ends, but any needle long enough to reach through will do. Put on several turns of thread, then tension as required before typing under the bottom button (FIG. 6-4K). One advantage of using a pin instead of a button is that it can be used to twist the thread to adjust tension. However, too much reliance should not be put on this, as excessive turning of the top button will eventually alter the tension.

If the inside would benefit by some padding—thin foam plastic may be fixed with adhesive to hardboard (or even card); this then is covered with lining cloth, which is turned under and tacked through (FIG. 6-4L). Adhesive may be used on the cloth edge before tacking.

7

Room Dividers

MUCH BUILT-IN FURNITURE goes flat against a wall or into a recess. This is a good way of utilizing space, which is often the main reason for building in furniture. An alternative use of built-in furniture comes when a room has to be divided, but without the drastic division that would come from building a wall.

A shelved room divider can separate parts of a room used for different purposes: A study area can be kept apart from the more general living area; the area used for eating can be divided from the part used for relaxing. This can be done without making too complete a barrier, particularly if the shelves are arranged to be accessible from both sides. In a large room such an arrangement allows for dual use without people in the two parts being out of touch with each other.

The divider could also serve as a display space or breakfast area. It might accommodate books, a radio, a tape recorder, or other items. If the lower part is enclosed with doors, it can be used for storage of things that would not be put on display.

PLANNING

It is not always easy to visualize how a divider or projecting block of shelves will look, and sometimes a final assembly of a different size is better than what was first planned. A shelf a little wider might be better for a record player; a projecting length a little less might make movement less restricted; a working surface might be better higher or lower.

Making a drawing to scale, with a section of the room included, will give some idea of sizes and the appearance and effect of the divider. Where possible, it is helpful to make a mockup. This can be made of cardboard, boxes, existing furniture, spare strips of wood—anything that you can put in position to indicate size and shape.

Manufactured boards are particularly suitable for dividers and shelves, so if you are able to use stock sizes, the actual construction will be simplified. The convenience of this will have to be balanced against the intended use of the divider and the floor space allocated. Planning is even more important in building something to project into the room than for furniture for against a wall.

CONFIGURATIONS OF DIVIDERS

Many great possibilities exist with divider construction. The basic divider can be regarded as a block of shelves fixed to the floor and one wall and projecting part way across a room (FIG. 7-1A). This may be entirely open shelving, or the lower part may be enclosed with doors (FIG. 7-1B). The

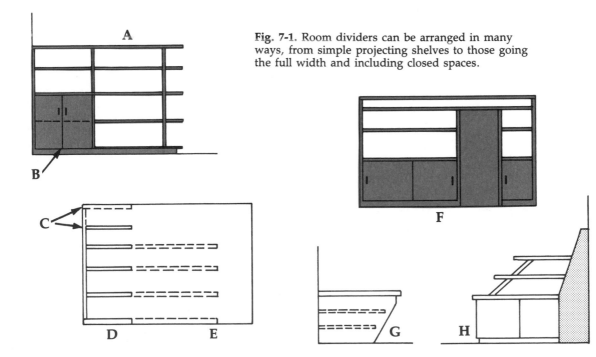

Fig. 7-1. Room dividers can be arranged in many ways, from simple projecting shelves to those going the full width and including closed spaces.

divider may go to the ceiling and be fixed to it, or it may be lower (FIG. 7-1C). It might go only a short way into the room to form a decorative feature without having much dividing effect (FIG. 7-1D), or it might go so far that only a small space is left to pass around the end (FIG. 7-1E).

It is also possible to let the divider go right across a room and allow a doorway at some intermediate point (FIG. 7-1F). The divider can be cut off at a working height for activities in a children's room or to serve as a bar (FIG. 7-1G). There can be some existing buttress, fireplace, or other projection that can be continued (FIG. 7-1H).

Another possibility is a divider with shelves open to both sides so things can be reached from either side and people in the two parts of the room can communicate with each other. If more privacy is desired, shelves can have enclosed backs. The reverse side can have covering to match the room walls and can be decorated with pictures or used as a notice or display board.

With wide shelves, privacy can be provided with dividing panels along the centers of the shelves; then the shelves can be used for different things on opposite sides. This is a particularly useful device for books, as a row of books is not very attractive from behind.

If there are doors over the lower shelves, they can come on one or both sides. If they are on one side, the other side should have a fixed back, which can extend behind the display shelves if privacy is wanted.

Drawers can be included, too. If a working top is to be used for eating and drinking, there can be a cutlery drawer, which can open from one side in the usual way or can be made to slide to either side.

You could add a complete block of drawers working in this way, but there are difficulties in providing stops, so you run a risk of a drawer being inadvertently pulled completely out. If the divider is being used as a bench for model making or some other activity that requires many tools, drawers are convenient.

DESIGNING THE DIVIDER FOR THE ROOM

The design of a divider or block of shelves must be related to the rest of the room and its contents. Consider lighting, both natural and artificial. Electrical lighting can be rearranged if necessary, but natural light from windows cannot usually be altered. If there are two or more windows, an open-shelved divider is unlikely to result in any unacceptably dark areas; but the availability of natural light must be considered, particularly if window area is small or a mostly enclosed divider is planned.

If you want a divider to "look light," design it so that closed parts are low and the shelf spacing decreases with height (FIG. 7-2A). Making higher

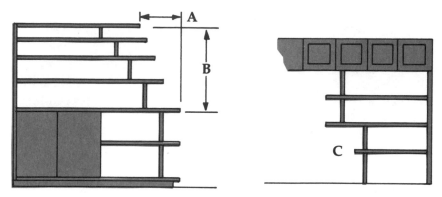

Fig. 7-2. Divider design considerations. For a light appearance, decrease shelf spacing with height (A) and make higher shelves shorter (B). For a look of solidity, use high doors and make high parts wider than lower parts (C).

shelves shorter also lightens appearance (FIG. 7-2B). Using light-colored wood or paint also helps. If more than one color is involved, the lighter color should be above the other.

If you want an effect of solidity or heaviness, possibly in contrast to a very lightly decorated room, you can add high doors (FIG. 7-2C) with upper parts longer than lower parts.

SIMPLE DIVIDER

The construction of a divider with an enclosed lower part and a few shelves is straightforward (FIG. 7-3). Exposed ends, particularly at the levels where anyone passing might touch them, should be rounded (FIG. 7-4A). This means that if you use prepared veneered or plastic surfaces boards, you should also use matching veneer to cover the shaped ends. Alternatively you could add molding around the end. To maintain the design feature, higher shelves should also be shaped, although if they are set back, they can be cut square across.

The bottom should be raised on a plinth (FIG. 7-4B), or short legs (FIG. 7-4C). The legs should lift the bottom high enough for cleaning beneath. It is preferable to use a matching board up the wall, with shelves doweled or fitted into dado joints (FIG. 7-4D); but each shelf may be bracketed to the wall, particularly if the wall covering seems more effective if carried right through (FIG. 7-4E).

In any case the attachment of the shelves at the wall end should be very secure. The base can be screwed to the floor, but if the top does not go to the ceiling, loads or shocks on most parts of the divider will be transmitted to fastenings at the wall end of the shelving.

In some circumstances there can be a solid upright at the free end of the divider. This adds rigidity, but it seems more appropriate for library

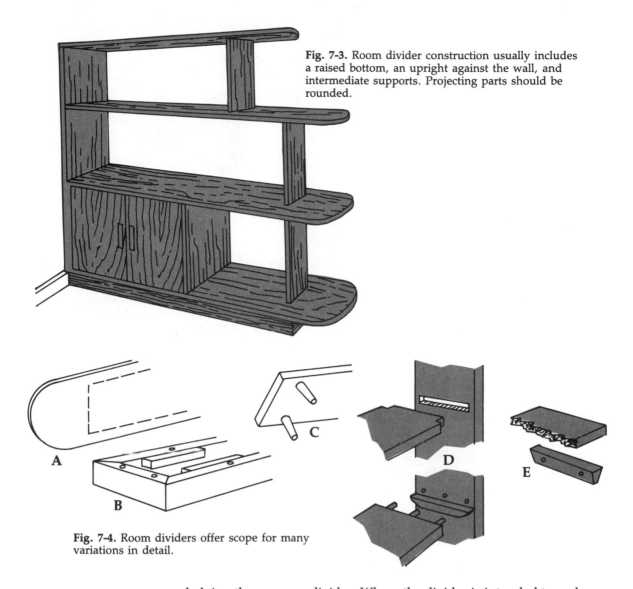

Fig. 7-3. Room divider construction usually includes a raised bottom, an upright against the wall, and intermediate supports. Projecting parts should be rounded.

Fig. 7-4. Room dividers offer scope for many variations in detail.

shelving than a room divider. Where the divider is intended to make an almost wall-like division between two areas, a solid end might be appropriate, and it should certainly be used if a door or screen will be attached.

The alternatives at the end are many. You could use pieces of the same section as the shelves, either doweled or dadoed. As it is difficult to get a series of short pieces precisely in line above each other and slight discrepancies will be rather obvious, it is better to stagger positions (FIG. 7-5A). If shelves are more than about 3 feet long, particularly if they are to be heavily loaded, intermediate supports are advisable.

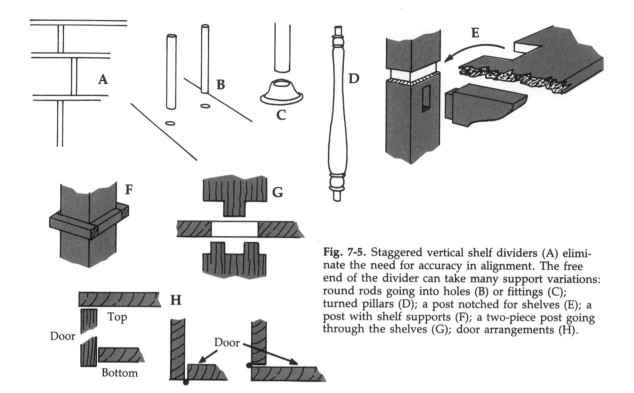

Fig. 7-5. Staggered vertical shelf dividers (A) eliminate the need for accuracy in alignment. The free end of the divider can take many support variations: round rods going into holes (B) or fittings (C); turned pillars (D); a post notched for shelves (E); a post with shelf supports (F); a two-piece post going through the shelves (G); door arrangements (H).

A lighter and more airy effect comes from using pillars. They can be plain round rods, located by holes at their ends (FIG. 7-5B) or taken into metal fittings or turned wood pieces (FIG. 7-5C). If you want to use standard pillars, buy them first thing, as their size can affect shelf spacing. Anyone with a lathe can make his or her own pillars (FIG. 7-5D), giving a more individual effect to the divider.

Another possibility is to use a single, fairly substantial post at one side. Then shelves are notched into it and brackets are tenoned in to support the width (FIG. 7-5E). You could then take the post centrally through the shelves. Then cut the shelves away to pass around it, and fix supporting pieces below (FIG. 7-5F). An alternative is to make the post in pieces with interconnected tenons (FIG. 7-5G).

Doors can fit between uprights or overlap them, but the shelf above a door should overhang it. It might be better to have the door above the bottom shelf than to cut the shelf back to allow the door to overlap (FIG. 7-5H). At the wall end the doorpost should be a few inches wide so the door opens well clear of the wall.

BAR WITH DRAWERS

A bar-type divider has a practical use. It allows people on one side to see into the other part of the room, yet it serves as a recognized partition: those preparing food can use the bar as a means of keeping others from interfering. As the bar will usually be used with high stools, the height should be decided by experimentation, but 36 inches is reasonable.

The top can be covered with Formica and edged with a metal molding. You could include one or two drawers, and the front might slope back to increase foot space (see FIG. 7-6).

As with a divider, the attachment to the wall should be strong. As the back will not normally be visible from the front, it might be solid wood, blockboard, or particleboard without veneer. The outer end is also solid, and it may have shelves built on to it (FIG 7-7A).

Put rails at the bottom drawer level (FIG. 7-7B) and arrange runners and kickers between them (FIG. 7-7C). Make sure opposite sides match and the drawers are at right angles to the sides if they are to be openable from both sides.

Plywood can be used for the sloping front. If you have shelves at the other side and the plywood is fixed to them, this will brace the bar, and

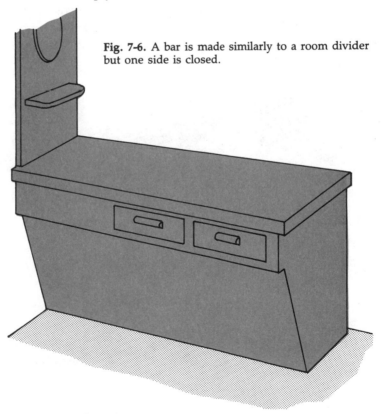

Fig. 7-6. A bar is made similarly to a room divider but one side is closed.

the plywood will be adequately stiffened (FIG. 7-7D).

Instead of plywood, the front might be made of hardboard that is fluted or decorated in some other way. However, hardboard is not as able to stand up to kicks, which it may get accidentally. Another possibility is to use wallpaper or upholstering on the front.

If the bar is to be used for hot food or alcoholic drinks, it will need a surface that will stand up to these things. There are plastic surfaces with wood grain effects that match the wood in the bar. The edge can be thickened and Formica or other plastic taken around it to show a more substantial edge (FIG. 7-7E).

Drawers have to be made with two fronts. Of course, the fronts cannot overlap, as the drawers are to slide through both ways. Sides can be dovetailed to the fronts or, more simply, rabbeted (FIG. 7-8A).

A plywood bottom can be slid into grooves before the second side is fitted to the fronts (FIG. 7-8B), or strips used inside (FIG. 7-8C). These strips at the sides also increase the bearing area of the drawer on the runners and reduce wear—which might be important if you expect the drawer to get a lot of use. Make sure the bottom edges of the fronts and any strips fixed to them do not project as low as the sides, otherwise they can catch on framing and interfere with the smooth action of the drawer.

In some situations the wall end of the bar can be continued upward, even as far as the ceiling. It can then be fitted with shelves or hooks for mugs. It might carry a mirror (FIG. 7-8D) or pictures.

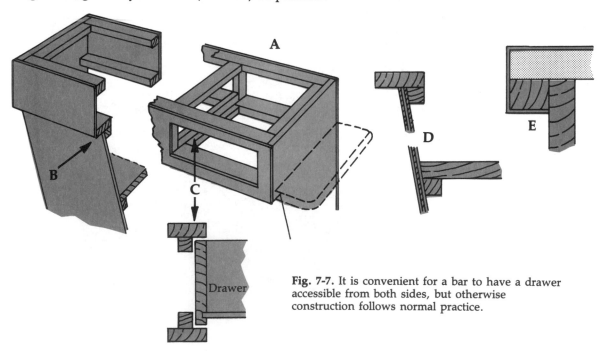

Fig. 7-7. It is convenient for a bar to have a drawer accessible from both sides, but otherwise construction follows normal practice.

Fig. 7-8. Drawer components in the bar may be dovetailed (A) or rabbeted (B); strips inside (C) will help reduce wear. The wall end of the bar can be extended upward to provide decoration or storage space (D).

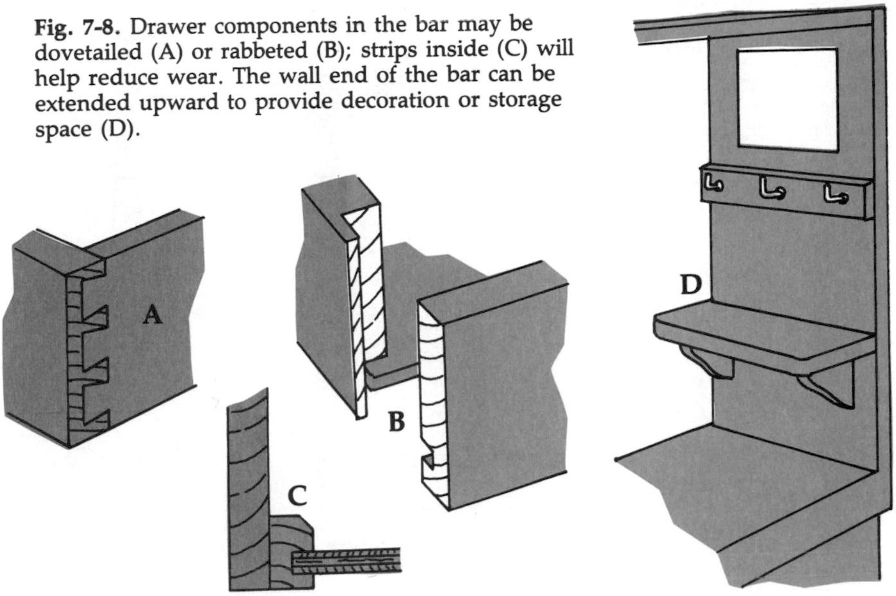

DIVIDER WITH TABLE

A divider might also incorporate other things. There can be a flap to swing down to form a writing desk, with compartments for stationery hidden behind it. A cocktail cabinet can be built in. A stereo system can be permanently installed, with speakers at the ends of the divider.

To include a table at a useful height, there has to be a part at about 30 inches above the floor (FIG. 7-9) big enough to provide space for the table. How the rest of the divider is made depends on requirements; it could be made in any of the ways already suggested, but the example shown provides some more ideas.

The main part of the divider is made as already described, with shelves securely fixed into the uprights. It can be treated as a unit, except for the extension of the top. The tabletop is round, with a center part wide enough to overlap the divider shelf sufficiently for the extension pieces to hang down when not required (FIG. 7-10A). Although it could be made from solid wood, it is probably better made of blockboard or particleboard with a suitable veneer.

At the center there should be a bolt to pass down through the shelf. The bolthead can be recessed into the wood and secured with a plate. The bolthead must be prevented from turning. If it is carefully set into the wood, that might provide sufficient grip, or it can be brazed or welded to the plate. A locknut keeps the bolt from loosening.

To ensure smooth action affix a piece of stout cloth, plastic, or rubber sheeting with adhesive under the tabletop (FIG. 7-10B). This can cover the

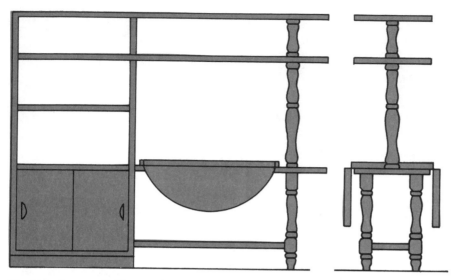

Fig. 7-9. A room divider can be embellished by turning. This divider includes a round folding table in the unit.

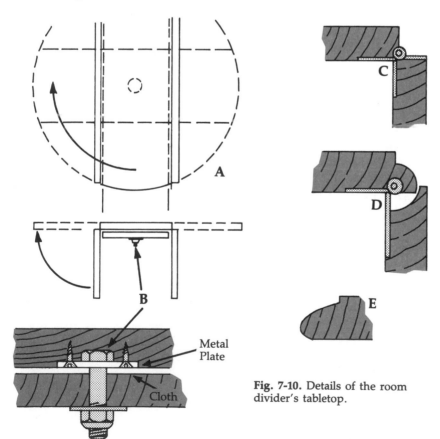

Metal Plate

Cloth

Fig. 7-10. Details of the room divider's tabletop.

part of the shelf that will be under the tabletop; or there can be a piece of about a 6-inch diameter around the bolt, and strips farther out towards the circumference of the tabletop. Having separate pieces is best if the hinges project at all under the top.

The hinges should be *back flaps*. These will swing back more than normal hinges so the table flaps can hang down (FIG. 7-10C).

Traditional drop-leaf tables have the meeting edges worked with a *rule joint* molding (FIG. 7-10D). (This can be done in solid wood, but manufactured boards cannot be shaped satisfactorily in this way.) If you want rule-joint molding, the total effect is improved if the table edge is also molded (FIG. 7-10E). To bring the table into use, the flaps are lifted and the top turned through a right angle.

In the example the shelf supporting the table has rails underneath and two legs. The legs can be square, preferably with a slight taper, but turned legs complement the round tabletop (FIG. 7-11A). The legs are joined with a lower piece that takes the end of a central rail. This allows more leg room for anyone sitting at the table than if the divider had been continued full width.

What comes above the table depends on the design and size of the divider. If it is not very high, there need be nothing extending from the main block. A shelf extending above the table without plenty of clearance might seem overpowering, but if the total height is perhaps 5 feet, it is

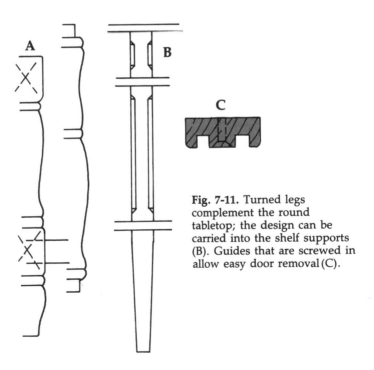

Fig. 7-11. Turned legs complement the round tabletop; the design can be carried into the shelf supports (B). Guides that are screwed in allow easy door removal (C).

possible to let the top extend and have another shelf below it. A pillar to support these shelves should carry through the design of the legs (FIG. 7-11B).

In the example sliding doors are shown. They could be plywood or glass. Sliding doors are often more convenient than swinging doors if space near the divider is restricted. However, swinging doors give better access to the interior, as sliding doors never expose more than half the inside.

For sliding doors in anything except the smallest sizes, it is best to buy a suitable door track and guides made of metal or plastic. Such guides provide a smoother action than anything that can be made from wood. If guides are made, pieces of hardwood can be grooved and screwed in place (FIG. 7-11C); then if the doors have to be removed, the screws can be withdrawn to release the guides.

Door edges, whether wood or glass, should be smooth and their corners rounded. The grooves should be sanded smooth and lubricated either with graphite (the end of a pencil) or candle wax—not oil or grease.

Although our ancestors probably never thought of room dividers, the effect of this piece of furniture with a round tabletop and turned legs and pillar is Jacobean. If this theme is to be carried through, the finish should be brown oak.

CLOSED BACKS

In most pieces of furniture the back is hidden and little care is lavished on its finish. If a divider is to have one side closed, the exposed side of the back paneling is at least as important as the side with shelves and doors. If it is to be hidden by wallpaper, it need not be of select veneer,

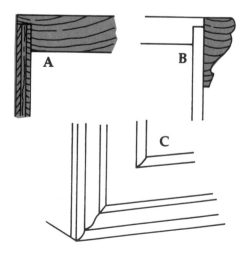

Fig. 7-12. A rabbeted joint at the top rear edge of the divider hides the plywood (A); the back can be made more attractive with molding (B). A paneled appearance could be obtained by using another molding (C).

but it should be flat and smooth. Even then, something might have to be done to break up the plainness of the surface.

At the top and wall edges the plywood can merely overlap, but anywhere that this joint would show the edge of the plywood, it is best to have a rabbet (FIG. 7-12A).

The plainness of the back can be broken up by using moldings. You can cover the edge with molding, using mitered corners (FIG. 7-12B). If the finish is polish or varnish over veneer, a paneled appearance can be obtained by using another light molding (FIG. 7-12C).

Of course, there are other uses for a plain back. If there is a study or working area behind the divider, the back can have shelves and racks to suit what is being done there. In a bedroom this might be a place to hang clothing.

A divider gives the opportunity for a lot of new thinking about a room, and its design offers plenty of opportunity to express individuality.

8

Kitchen Furniture

WITH ALL OF THE EQUIPMENT that goes into a modern kitchen, any built-in furniture has to be planned to fill gaps rather than provide the main furnishing. Fortunately most kitchen equipment is now made to a standard height, which simplifies matching appliances with built-in items. If built-in furniture is to be used in a new kitchen, there are more possibilities for planning than there would be with an existing kitchen.

It is helpful, with a new kitchen, to have a scale drawing of the floor plan, with windows, heaters, and doors marked. Cut out, to scale, card shapes of the things in the room and move these around to try various layouts. Consider heights. Be careful that a high item does not come where it would shield the light from some other item.

Normally the size of the room only allows the fixed items to be placed around the walls, but if you have enough space, it might be helpful to allow a working top or some other floor-standing item project into the room. This can be used as a breakfast bar or a room divider.

Before building everything in tightly, consider the ventilation requirements of appliances. Also, there must be space for fresh room air to be admitted and used air exhausted.

The neatest and most practical arrangement is to have front edges in line, so it might be necessary to build out anything that is shallow or recessed. However, if the kitchen is small and every inch of open floor space is valuable, it might be better to set things back as close to the wall as possible and let the front edges come as they will. The item that projects most should be placed toward the end rather than near the center of a wall so as to be less of a hazard to anyone passing by it. If there is a piece of floor-standing equipment that is only occasionally used, it might be best to have it under a fixed top for storage.

If you can plan the kitchen as a whole, you can give it a pleasing appearance by using matching colors, worktop finishes, and handles throughout. With existing equipment installed, some differences might have to be accepted.

The best use of space is usually achieved by having the working surfaces uncluttered and back toward the wall, with enough space above them to admit the usual mixers, pots and pans, and other things used in food preparation. Farther up the wall there can be storage shelves and cupboards. These should have their bases high enough so as not to obscure the view of the working tops, and they should usually not project as far from the wall as the working tops.

After trying various layouts with card cutouts on a scale drawing, sketch the arrangements on the walls (FIG. 8-1A). Even better, if you can imagine it, try to depict appearances pictorially (FIG. 8-1B).

The actual construction of built-in items for a kitchen can be much the same as for cabinets already described, but some specific suggestions are given next. Although many items can be made as units—and they might have to be if a stove or other item comes between built-in items—it is always better to carry through such things as the rails under the front of a top to ensure uniformity and stability.

SINK UNIT

The sink unit will usually determine the design pattern for other built-ins, so it should be made first. Obtain the top first and plan the woodwork to suit it. A common arrangement has drawers and doors below the top. Although there cannot be a drawer at the sink position, a dummy drawer front might be located there for appearance (FIG. 8-2A).

Before planning the details of construction, the plumbing layout should be settled. With a little readjustment to the framing at the back of the unit, the amount of cutting away for pipes can be reduced. The wall can form the back of the unit, which will simplify plumbing; but if the wall is uneven, it is better to have a plywood or hardboard back.

Arrange the bottom of the unit a few inches above the floor to allow for a plinth (FIG. 8-2B). There can be solid wood under the doors, and plywood farther back. Although thinner plywood can be used for divisions and the outside casing, heavy items might be stored under the

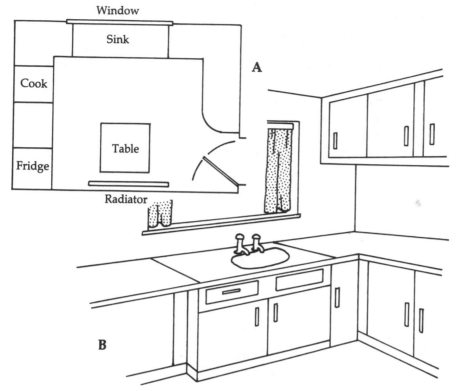

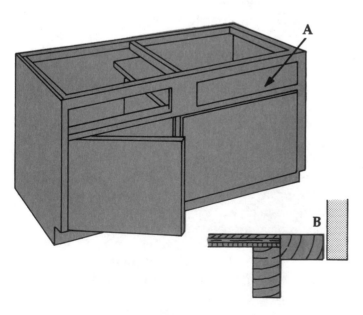

Fig. 8-1. The floor plan shows the arrangement of kitchen units at working level. The pictorial rendition shows the higher storage units as well.

Fig. 8-2. A basic construction plan for kitchen cabinets. The sink part has a matching front panel (A). Doors may overlap the bottom (B). A central divider also supports a shelf (C and D).

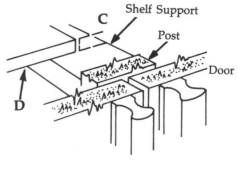

sink, and it is advisable to use plywood not less than ⅜ of an inch thick for the bottom.

Doors may overlap the sides and either meet at a post or overlap one (FIG. 8-2C). In any case, the post will also take the end of a shelf support. The shelf might come just above half the internal height, and it is usually better to keep it back a few inches from the doors (FIG. 8-2D). If you use plywood, thicken the front and add a support along and under the back.

Ends can be plywood or hardboard framed inside. Drawers can be made in any of the ways described earlier. Wood or metal door slides are satisfactory.

How the top is fixed depends on its design. A metal top can come with its edge turned under. This can be allowed to hang over the front, but at the ends and back it is better to either make a rabbet around the top edge of the wood or build up the parts to suit (FIG. 8-3). If you provide screw holes, screws can be used; but if the woodwork is made to push fit into the metal edges and jointing compound or mastic is used to bed the top down, there should be no need for screws.

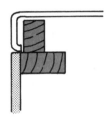

Fig. 8-3. The metal covering on the worktop overhangs built-up sections at the unit's ends and back.

Complete all internal work before affixing the top, including painting and checking the fit and action of the drawers. Make a trial assembly of the doors, then remove them and their fittings for painting.

KITCHEN STORAGE UNITS

A cabinet can be made the same way as the sink unit, but with a particle board or blockboard top covered with Formica. This should match the sink unit and other items. If any clamp-on kitchen device is to be used, make sure that the top is not too thick for the clamps. The top looks better if it is thickened slightly, and this gives a better gluing area for edging strips of Formica (FIG. 8-4A).

If the back of the unit is to be open to the wall, it is usually best to start by making up the front of the unit together with an end. Use a straightedge and spirit level with these parts to define points where the top edge of wall battens should come, then affix these parts to the wall (FIG. 8-4B).

If a washing machine, dryer, or other equipment that has to be moved is to be housed under the working top, the floor will have to be the bottom

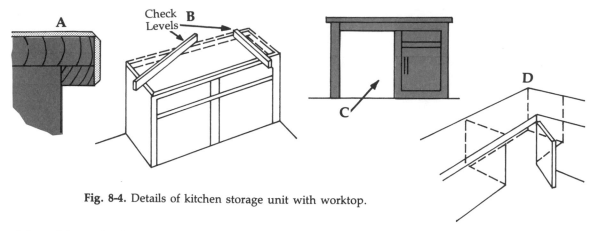

Fig. 8-4. Details of kitchen storage unit with worktop.

of the cabinet. Or the unit can have one part with a bottom and another part open to the floor. There can be a door where the movable machine goes, or the front can be left open (FIG. 8-4C).

A worktop in a corner is convenient as a working area, but access to all of the space underneath is not always easy to arrange. If a one storage unit comes up to the corner, the other overlaps its end and there is no direct access to the corner (FIG. 8-4D). This is probably the best place to store something that has to pull out. Less frequently used items also can go in the corner.

KITCHEN WALL STORAGE

Many kitchen implements can be hung from the wall or put on shelves. To a certain extent, hanging items can be regarded as decorative. A rail with a row of hooks is preferable to hooks attached directly to the wall. The top of the rail should slope so it does not collect dust. A piece of veneered or Formica-covered manufactured board, or plain wood finished with gloss paint or varnish, can be used.

Perforated hardboard can be held off the wall with battens so hooks can be put through the holes. This allows a convenient change of layout. Shelves should be given a Formica finish for the sake of appearance and hygiene.

The kitchen looks neater if most things are hidden in drawers or behind doors. There is usually space along the wall, in the angle between wall and ceiling for a cupboard. Cupboard storage can extend from the ceiling down to a point that does not interfere with use of the worktop. It is usually possible to make the bottom shelf reachable from the floor. Doors may either swing or slide, but sliding doors are more suitable for long cupboards than for narrow ones (FIG. 8-5A).

Arrange swinging doors so they give the most convenient access. This could mean an end door swinging toward the wall with the next door

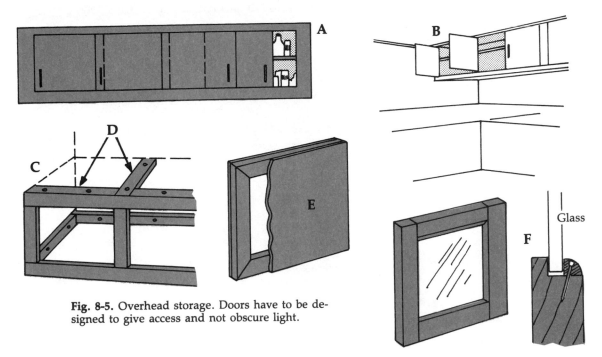

Fig. 8-5. Overhead storage. Doors have to be designed to give access and not obscure light.

swinging the same way if it comes over a working surface in a corner (FIG. 8-5B).

A high cupboard can be simply framed (FIG. 8-5C) and the walls and ceiling used for sides, so not much material is required. However, the strain on fastenings can be considerable when the shelves are fully loaded, so provide plenty of support (FIG. 8-5D).

The doors can be plywood or hardboard on strip wood (FIG. 8-5E). Except for large doors, there should be no need for intermediate strips.

An alternative is to have glass panels. There may be glass sliding doors, or a wood door can be made as a frame to take glass (FIG. 8-5F). In the latter case, use a rabbet and hold the glass in with a bead. Then, if the glass has to be replaced, this can be done without damaging the door.

Glass doors allow things to be seen through them and allow light to pass through. In some situations opening a solid door blocks the light from the working area.

COMBINED KITCHEN CABINETS

In a very small kitchen there might be some advantage in letting one unit go from floor to ceiling (FIG. 8-6A). The whole assembly is basically a working top with storage underneath, but with its sides going up to support the upper storage shelves or cupboards. This relieves the wall and ceiling of much of the load and is a good idea if you are doubtful about the holding power of these parts.

There can also be narrow shelves at the back (FIG. 8-6B) with hooks for cups inside the uprights. Of course, the working area is limited, but this unit will make the most use of available space.

Another possibility is a drop-front working area. This can come as part of a large block of storage space (FIG. 8-7A) or it can be part of a shallower tall cabinet in a very tiny kitchen (Such as the one shown in FIG. 8-6).

The front could swing down on hinges or one long piano hinge (FIG. 8-7B), or it could pivot on metal rods through the sides (FIG. 8-7C). The

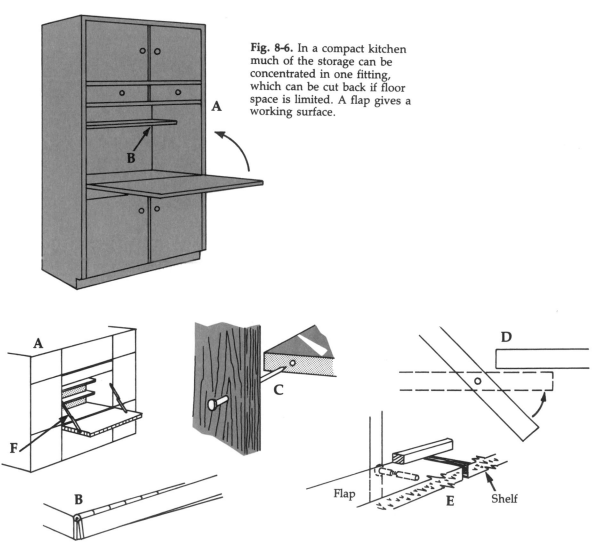

Fig. 8-6. In a compact kitchen much of the storage can be concentrated in one fitting, which can be cut back if floor space is limited. A flap gives a working surface.

Fig. 8-7. The drop-front working area could be part of a large storage unit (A). It could swing down on hinges (B), pivot on a rod (C), swing under a shelf (D), or it could be supported by stops on uprights (E). Folding stays at the sides give added strength (F).

front could swing under the shelf (FIG. 8-7D), or it could be flush with the shelf so stops on the uprights hold it in the down position (FIG. 8-7E). In a small cabinet the overlap of the flap with the shelf or stops might be stiff enough to withstand working loads on the front, but there could be folding stays at the sides as well (FIG. 8-7F).

The lower part of this unit can have open shelves or doors, but in a very confined space the sides might have to be cut back to allow for foot space (FIG. 8-8).

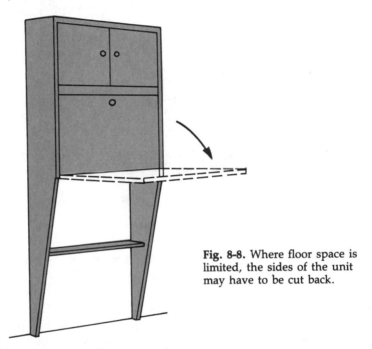

Fig. 8-8. Where floor space is limited, the sides of the unit may have to be cut back.

The hinged flap is best made of particleboard with Formica on both sides and preferably around the edges. Ball catches may be used at each side to hold the flap up.

The inside of the unit should be painted a light color. The outside can be painted to match the inside or surrounding colors, but avoid a dark color on a small unit, as this would make it seem even smaller.

There can also be spaces to fill between the sides of kitchen equipment. These may be only a few inches wide, but they should be closed to give a uniform appearance around the walls. Filler pieces can be made to match the built-in furniture and can merely press into place so it is easy to remove them if an appliance has to be withdrawn for servicing.

9

Space Savers

BUILT-IN ITEMS can be useful and decorative in confined spaces. These items also provide an opportunity to use up leftovers from larger projects.

These smaller items may come flat against a wall or worked into a corner beside a door. They can occupy a small recess or other place too narrow for a freestanding piece of furniture. If they are fixed to the wall and do not reach the floor, they do not restrict walking space. In general, the attraction of small built-in items is in utilizing small spaces.

The design of space-economizing built-in furniture is very dependent on actual situations, so many variations are possible. The amount of projection from a wall may be governed by the distance from the wall to the edge of a doorway in a corner. The location of a mirror might be determined by the available light and how far it is possible to stand from the mirror in a narrow passage. Any shelving may have to suit particular items that will stand on it. The suggestions given next can be adapted to suit these and other circumstances.

HALL MIRRORS

A mirror near an outside door allows anyone passing in or out to make a quick check on his or her appearance. It can include some provision for hair and clothes brushes and perhaps coat hooks.

Mirrors with Shelves

A simple mirror with a shelf is shown in FIG. 9-1A. The exposed edges are cut with curves, which give a more graceful effect than straight lines. As the mirror determines the sizes of other parts, this should be obtained first. Suggested sizes are given. It is possible to frame the top of the mirror. Otherwise the exposed mirror edges should be ground and polished.

The sides (FIG. 9-1B) are cut with two rabbets—one for the mirror and one for the backing plywood. This makes it possible to affix the assembly to the wall without the glass, using screws through the plywood, and then slide the mirror in from the top. If there is not enough clearance to do this, the mirror may be inserted before fixing to the wall and some brass mirror plates used at the sides. The glass makes the unit quite heavy for its size. There should be two or more stout screws fairly high and one or more farther down.

The shelf can be fitted into a dado joint at each end (FIG. 9-1C). Dowels can also be used, and a simple template (FIG. 9-1D) can be used to make the holes.

A filler piece (FIG. 9-1E) goes below the mirror and shelf. The plywood backing can be cut to match the top of the mirror or can be taken straight across between the sides (FIG. 9-1F). Check that the rabbets for the glass will allow it to slide in easily yet be free from wobble after it is inserted. Then stain and varnish the woodwork. If there is any risk of dampness, a coat of varnish on the back of the mirror itself will reduce the risk of moisture damage to the silvering.

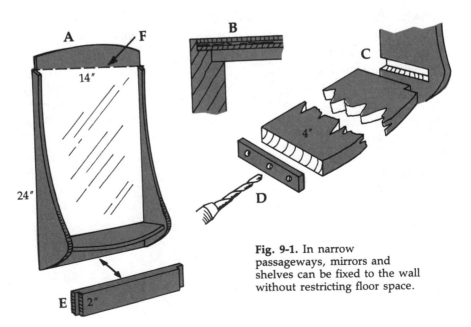

Fig. 9-1. In narrow passageways, mirrors and shelves can be fixed to the wall without restricting floor space.

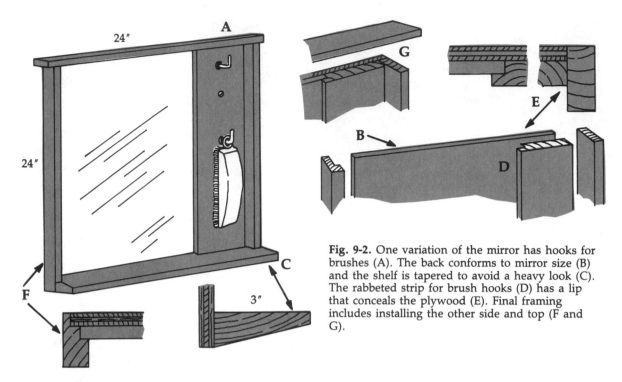

Fig. 9-2. One variation of the mirror has hooks for brushes (A). The back conforms to mirror size (B) and the shelf is tapered to avoid a heavy look (C). The rabbeted strip for brush hooks (D) has a lip that conceals the plywood (E). Final framing includes installing the other side and top (F and G).

A variation on this (FIG. 9-2A) involves hooks for brushes. It can be made in the same way as the first mirror, with extra backing at one side. The simple design shown gets its beauty from the grain of the wood rather than shaping of the sides.

The basic part is the plywood back. The shape of the back is determined by the size of the mirror (FIG. 9-2B). The shelf is thickened at the back for stiffness. Tapering from below avoids a heavy look (FIG. 9-2C).

The strip for the brush hooks has a rabbet to suit the glass (FIG. 9-2D). A lip on its edge covers the plywood and provides a support for the top (FIG. 9-2E). At the opposite side a rabbeted strip projects the same amount (FIG. 9-2F). The single rabbet is sufficiently deep for the glass as well as the plywood.

The top is a strip of wood that fits over side strips and the back after the glass has been fitted (FIG. 9-2G). Mounting is done with screws through the plywood.

If there is insufficient space above to slide the mirror in after the woodwork has been fixed to the wall, the assembly can be made to swing if one of the upper screws is through the side wood. The screw that will come behind the glass is driven in, and the assembly is swung on this to allow the glass to be fitted (FIG. 9-3). Then the unit is positioned and the other screw is driven.

Fig. 9-3. If there is not enough clearance above the unit to allow sliding the mirror in from the top, the unit can be mounted so it pivots to allow the mirror to be installed from the side.

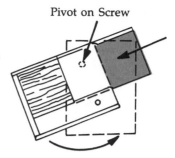

Pivot on Screw

Mirror With Clothes Hooks

Clothes hooks may be mounted on wings extending from each side of the mirror frame (FIG. 9-4A). The mirror is fully framed, and it can be held in place with a plywood back and fastenings in the same way a picture is framed (FIG. 9-4B).

The woodwork can be doweled together. The traditional method would be to use mortise and tenon joints (FIG. 9-4C), but it is possible to have some parts and supplement glue with screws driven from the back (FIG. 9-4D). Edges may be finished by working a mold around the outline if a power molding tool is available.

Coat hooks may be bought or can be wooden pegs turned on a lathe (FIG. 9-4E). Pieces of dowel could be inserted in holes at an angle. If the

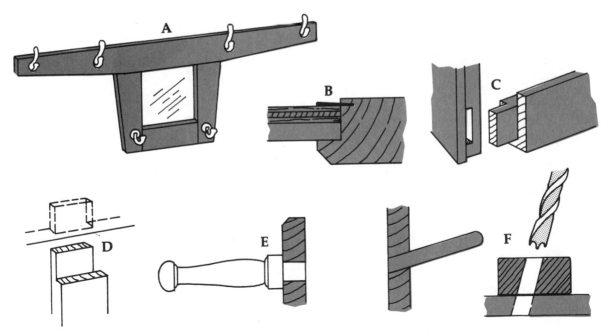

Fig. 9-4. A hall mirror can be extended to provide clothes-hanging space.

holes cannot be made on a drilling machine with a tilting table, the holes can be made at a uniform angle by drilling freehand through a block of wood with a suitable hole (FIG. 9-4F).

SHELVING

Shelves can be arranged to make use of space that would otherwise serve no purpose. A block of shelves can go along a wall from the corner by a door (FIG. 9-5A). The number of shelves and their size will depend on the situation, but a width to suit books is suitable for a living room.

For the design shown, construction can be made with either dado joints or dowels. If the uprights are narrower than the shelves (FIG. 9-5B), intermediate dado joints can go right through. Joints are stopped elsewhere (FIG. 9-5C). Having the piece at the door end narrower facilitates fitting against molding (FIG. 9-5D) and allows shelves a little wider than they could be otherwise.

In most places a plinth under the bottom shelf (FIG. 9-5E) is advisable, and there may be a plywood back with a covering strip above the top shelf (FIG. 9-5F) to protect the wall from articles on the shelf.

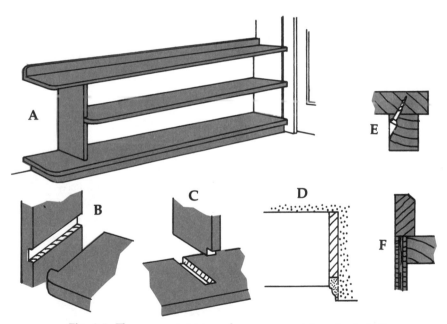

Fig. 9-5. The corner next to a doorway may take a bookshelf.

A similar arrangement can be used for the storage of cleaning tools (FIG. 9-6A). Hooks for hanging smaller brushes and other tools can be driven into uprights and other members. At the bottom there can be a rail to keep bottles and cans in place (FIG. 9-6B).

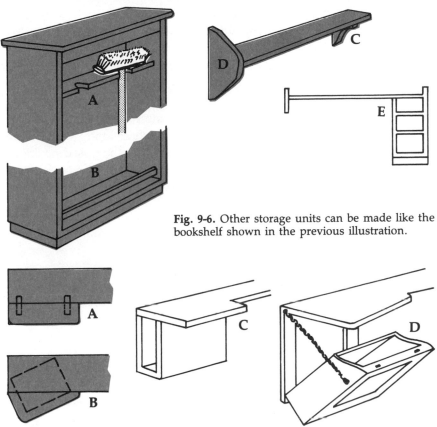

Fig. 9-6. Other storage units can be made like the bookshelf shown in the previous illustration.

Fig. 9-7. A shelf may be broadened to take a telephone (A) and have a bin below it for a directory (B through D).

Another convenient place for a shelf is above a radiator. There should be a gap of several inches to keep the shelf from becoming too hot.

The simplest shelf is a piece of wood on brackets (FIG. 9-6C). Wooden brackets look better than ordinary metal shelf brackets. End brackets may be extended as shown to keep from sliding off the ends (FIG. 9-6D). One end can extend into a block of shelves (FIG. 9-6E). Such a unit might be used below one of the mirrors already described. The single shelf could continue up into a block of shelves.

The shelf over a radiator could be extended for the telephone and its accessories. The telephone portion will have to be at least 5 inches wide. It can be built out with a piece glued on and possibly strengthened with dowels (FIG. 9-7A). The most compact arrangement has the telephone parallel with the wall, but if the extra projection will not matter, putting the telephone on an angle produces an interesting appearance (FIG. 9-7B). To prevent the instrument from being knocked off the shelf, drill holes to take its feet or strips or wood to form a frame around it.

One way of accommodating the directory and other papers is to make an open-sided compartment into which they can slide from the side, beneath the telephone shelf (FIG. 9-7C).

Another way is to make a box compartment that will tilt forward yet hide its contents when closed (FIG. 9-7D). A hanger is fixed to the wall and may hide one or more metal shelf brackets. The box is lightly made of plywood and may have its front framed to improve appearance. There are two hinges at the bottom of the back, and a chain limits swing. One or a pair of ball catches at the top will hold the box in the closed position.

WALL DRESSING TABLE

In the smallest bedrooms or those already full of furniture, the only way to fit in a dressing table is to keep it as shallow as possible and attach it from the wall. The accompanying mirror is fixed to the wall above the table and not attached to the table.

In one version (FIG. 9-8A), the top, which may be veneered or plastic-covered plywood or particleboard, is bracketed to the wall and given legs that taper back to provide minimum floor obstruction. There may be shelf as well. If there is a plywood back between the top and the shelf, this can be stiffened to take fastenings to the wall.

Doweled construction is best for particleboard. With solid wood you might use a dovetail dado joint between uprights and top (FIG. 9-8B), which will prevent warping. A simpler alternative is to use screwed and glued blocks on one or both sides of the uprights (FIG. 9-8C).

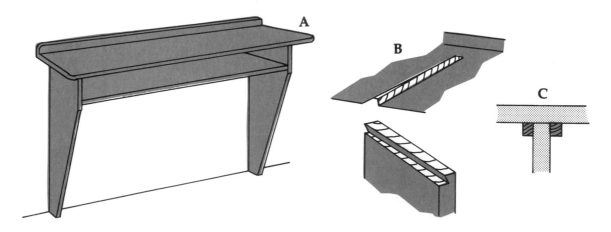

Fig. 9-8. In a small bedroom a dressing table can be arranged below a wall mirror. The table is supported so there is little obstruction at floor level.

Front edges can be molded or beveled. With this and other shelf assemblies at about waist level, it is always advisable to round projecting corners to minimize damage to the structure and any person bumping it.

A Lighter Dressing Table

If the theme of the room is airy and light, a more delicately framed structure is preferable. This can be achieved by using rods or legs instead of solid uprights. A plain top can be bracketed to the wall and given a drawer or shelf and round legs (FIG. 9-9A). There may be more legs and more shelves, or a broad shelf may take the place of the drawer.

The top can be bracketed, as in the other type, or there can be a backboard fixed to the wall and a batten below (FIG. 9-9B). Screws are driven from the batten into the top (FIG. 9-9C). As the legs will take much of the downward load, possible strain on wall fastenings is not as great.

The backs of lower shelves can also rest on battens (FIG. 9-9D). The legs can be prepared type with ferrules and end fittings. In that case their length may determine the height of the top. Alternatively, use dowel rods of about 1 inch diameter or make suitable legs on a lathe. At the lower shelf level the leg goes straight through. As the legs will take much of the downward load, possible strain on wall fastenings is not as great. A peg, preferably metal, goes through the leg to support the shelf, and a washer goes above that (FIG. 9-9E).

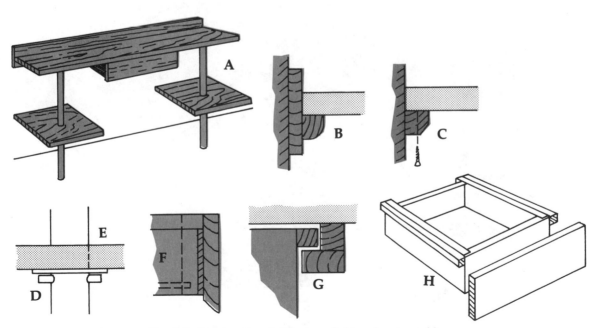

Fig. 9-9. Construction details for a lighter dressing table.

The drawer can have rabbeted lap joints (FIG. 9-9F). The bottom may be glued and nailed from below or recessed into grooves. If the drawer is set under the top and the facing extends below the front, there will be no need for a handle (FIG. 9-9G). The simplest way of hanging the drawer is to put runners along the top edges and make supports for these under the top (FIG. 9-9H).

BATHROOM FITTING

Although a bathroom is occupied only briefly, there are many toilet articles to be accommodated in a small room, and keeping all these things tidy means having quite compact fittings. A suggested bathroom fixture is shown in FIG. 9-10A.

Because of the damp atmosphere, the wood needs protection. This can be done with suitable paint. Plastic-covered manufactured board can also be used, providing it has waterproof glue holding the plastic laminations. It is also possible to use glass instead of wood for some shelves. This gives a hygienic appearance, as does a finish in a light pastel shade.

Although the fitting might have to be supported mainly by the wall, stronger support is obtained if you can take one or more parts to the floor. If one end is in a corner, additional fastenings through the end can provide more strength. Avoid plain iron or steel fastenings, as these have a tendency to rust.

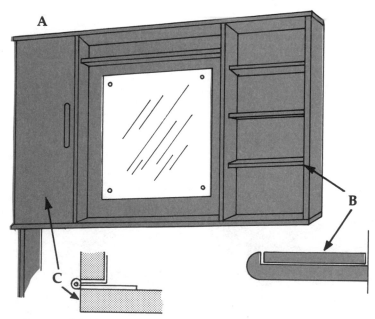

Fig. 9-10. In a small bathroom a mirror and storage fixture can be hung from the wall. A leg to the floor can give additional support.

Construction is by any of the usual methods. The mirror may be framed, or it could be fixed with domed-head screws through holes in the glass. The best place for a strip light is over the mirror. Glass shelves can rest on wooden brackets, preferably with front lips to keep the glass from sliding in (FIG. 9-10B). Metal fittings for glass shelves can be used. Some of these allow for adjustment to different heights, which may be an advantage if the storage arrangements are changed.

There are always a great many things in a bathroom that are better hidden, so a door over part of the fixture is a good idea (FIG. 9-10C). If this is kept tall and narrow, a stock size of particleboard may be used, hiding whatever number of shelves you include.

Other items can be hung outside the fixture, either with hooks or brackets, and towel rails can be slung underneath.

10

Fireside Fittings

A LIVING ROOM BENEFITS FROM having a focal point. In the days when the only means of heating was solid fuel burned in an open fire, the fireplace was the focal point. Modern central heating is very attractive, but it does not provide a focal point. Because of this, some homes still have a fireplace, even if for all practical purposes it is unnecessary.

A wall-mounted electric heater or a gas fire can also serve as a focal point. The electric heater might also produce a simulated log or coal fire that creates the right look even when heat is not needed. Such a unit's purpose as a focal point can be enhanced by building a furniture unit around it. The room is then planned so seating and activities in the room will be directed towards the wall with the heater. Anything built in should provide storage as well as decoration complementary to the use of the room. The design may vary from something compact, arranged in the immediate vicinity of the heater, to a complex fitting that covers the whole of a wall.

The built-in unit will usually be designed to suit the size of the heating unit. It may also be necessary to take into account access for maintenance. Cables, switches, and pipes should not be covered if they may have to be reached later. A small unit can be fixed to the wall with a few screws so it can be removed quickly if the heater has to be serviced. Access for servicing a larger unit while it is in position might need to be considered.

So that air can circulate around the heater, all woodwork should be kept away from it. How far depends on the particular unit, but 3 inches at the sides and 6 inches at the top are probable minimums. If the fitting projects far in front of the heater, any woodwork above might have to be cut back to allow hot air to rise and prevent the wood from getting too hot. Heating efficiency will be improved and the wood protected from overheating if a piece of metal, curved to throw the rising hot air forward, is mounted below the shelf and over the heater.

Whether to have a projection at floor level is a matter of personal preference. This dates from the days when burning coal or wood might fall out of the fire; a hearth was provided to catch it. Besides giving the traditional effect, a hearth prevents the unit from being kicked and helps to keep persons from getting too close to the heat source.

SIMPLE FIRE SURROUND

In this unit (FIG. 10-1), a mantel shelf joins two blocks of shelves at the sides, which may be used for books or ornaments. The heater is measured and sufficient clearance allowed. The top should usually be at least 30 inches from the floor, even if this causes a very wide gap above the heater. You might have enough space for another shelf below the top.

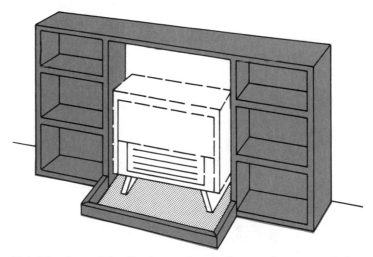

Fig. 10-1. The days of the fireplace and open fire may have passed, but an electric heater with storage shelves around it can provide a focal point in a room.

The shelf depth depends on the unit's purpose. Five inches is necessary for most books. Three inches may be right for ornaments, particularly in a small room, where too much projection might look overpowering.

Make a dimensioned sketch or a drawing showing the main lines to scale to see if proportions look right and to decide on the sizes of wood needed. If you use manufactured board you might be able to design a unit that requires stock sizes and avoid waste and unnecessary cuts.

If you have a base molding around the room, you might be able to cut it away. If not, the fitting must be cut around it. To prevent the edge of the plywood above the molding from warping, apply a piece of half-round or other molding (FIG. 10-2A).

Allow for a strip across the top (FIG. 10-2B) to support and stiffen the top. Rising hot air can cause light-sectioned solid wood to warp, so be sure to use not less than 1 inch thickness and to include a front stiffener if the central gap is more than about 2 feet (FIG. 10-2C). Manufactured board should not warp. Solid wood will not warp if a piece is chosen with the annual rings going across the thickness (FIG. 10-2D).

If you prefer solid wood and traditional methods, prepare for the back by rabbeting the parts where it will fit. The rear piece under the top may be rabbeted for the full length if this is easier, as the central rabbet is unlikely to show. Top corners can be dovetailed (FIG. 10-2E) with the inner uprights in dado joints and the rear strip passing through (FIG. 10-2F). Shelves are also fitted into dado grooves (FIG. 10-2G) The outer uprights can go into dovetail or rabbet joints (FIG. 10-2H).

In a simpler construction the joints are made with screwed blocks, which can be bought as plastic units or made from strip wood (FIG. 10-3A). The success of this construction depends on accurate cutting of ends. Neatness at the top corners is achieved if the top overlaps (FIG. 10-3B). Bottoms may be screwed into uprights. If the top is to be veneered, screws may be driven through the top into the uprights by counterbored holes and plugs with the screws.

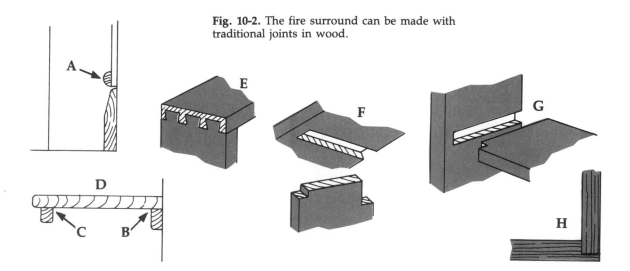

Fig. 10-2. The fire surround can be made with traditional joints in wood.

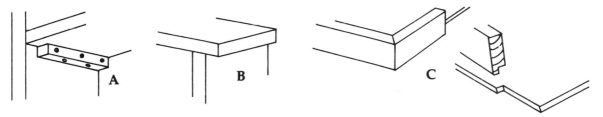

Fig. 10-3. If the surround is made of a manufactured board, simpler joints can be used.

If there is to be a base under the heater, this could be plywood covered with Formica. It should be fixed, but for convenience in cleaning, it should be removable. It can be made narrow enough to fit between the shelf units, or it can be cut back to butt against them (FIG. 10-3C). A similar idea can be used if the base is to run the full width of the unit, letting the wood sides of the base butt against the outer uprights.

LARGER SURROUND

The basic design can be extended outward and upward. The result might be an assembly of cupboards, shelves, and racks over an entire wall. Although such a design may be thought of as one unit, it is usually best to divide it into parts which are assembled separately and brought together. In this way, satisfactory construction is easier, and there is less risk of parts being out of square. With a single assembly involving many compartments, some part will not come to a right angle no matter what you do—probably due to an accumulation of small errors leading up to that point. This can be minimized if independent modules are made.

Although a large surround may consist entirely of shelves, it is usually better for convenience and appearance to provide doors so some of the shelves become closets. There may be a second shelf on top (FIG. 10-4).

Construction is generally similar to that of the simpler unit described earlier. In a traditional construction, the lower top may use a combination dado-and-dovetail joint (FIG. 10-5A). In the simpler construction, blocks below the shelf may be sufficient, although a dado adds strength (FIG. 10-5B). The lower top piece should be cut back over the heater to the same width as the upper piece (FIG. 10-5C).

If hinged doors are used, they may be placed between the uprights (FIG. 10-6A) or may overlap them (FIG. 10-6B). In any case, the shelf above the door should overlap it to keep out dust.

Small sliding doors may be glass or plywood in grooves. The grooves are best made by strips of wood glued in place. If the top groove is made deep enough, the door can be lifted out (FIG. 10-6C). For larger wooden doors it is advisable to use a sliding doortrack, as wood sliding on wood can offer too much resistance. Get the sliding-door fittings before settling

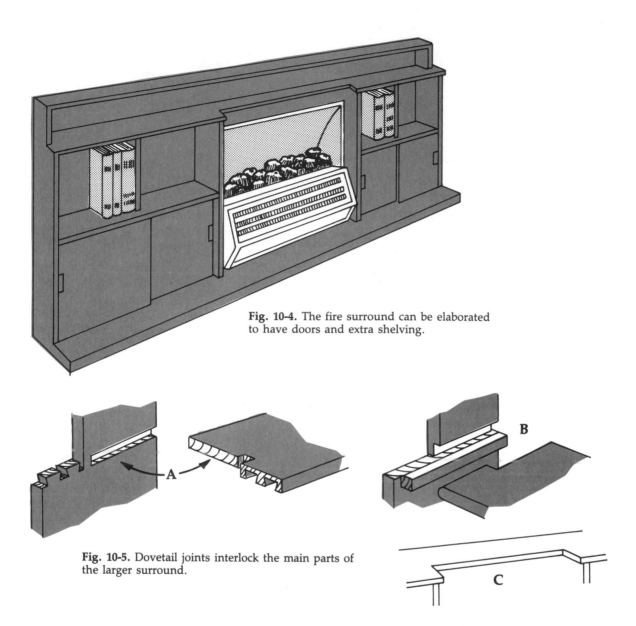

Fig. 10-4. The fire surround can be elaborated to have doors and extra shelving.

Fig. 10-5. Dovetail joints interlock the main parts of the larger surround.

the final sizes of the design, as it might be possible to modify the design slightly to suit the fittings.

With doors that reach to the bottom, the hearthlike bottom should have a flush top (FIG. 10-6D). A raised edge would necessitate having the door bottom high enough to swing over it. The bottom can be made with plywood supported by framing, using a strip under the closet fronts and sufficient cross members for stiffness (FIG. 10-6E).

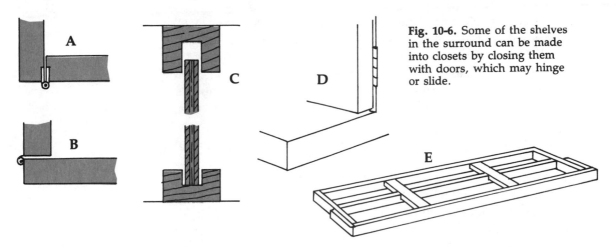

Fig. 10-6. Some of the shelves in the surround can be made into closets by closing them with doors, which may hinge or slide.

Of course, this unit can be modified in numerous ways. It need not be symmetrical. It could have a much larger extension on one side than the other. The purpose of each part could be adapted to match other furniture. If one side is near a sewing machine, for instance, that side can be entirely closed with doors for storage of sewing equipment; the other side might consist entirely of book shelves. There could be sliding doors at one side, hinged doors at the other side. The sliding doors could come above open shelves instead of below, especially if they are glass doors covering displayed items.

FOLDING SEAT

A heater surround can also incorporate a pair of folding stools that close into the unit and can be drawn out for use. Comfort controls sizes. In use the top should be 12 to 15 inches above the floor, so the hinge line should be at this height (FIG. 10-7A). It is possible to have the seat fold down, but it is easier to have it fold up. There must be enough height above the hinge line to allow for this, the height being the depth of the

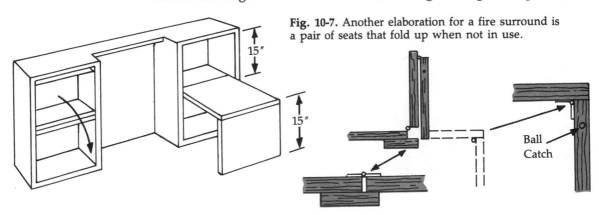

Fig. 10-7. Another elaboration for a fire surround is a pair of seats that fold up when not in use.

seat. For an overall height of 30 inches, this would be 15 inches (FIG. 10-7B). Although a wide seat might be most comfortable, having the width and height about the same allows the stool to fold inconspicuously (FIG. 10-7C).

The top of the stool and the front support can both be made of veneered manufactured board, or they can be blockboard with solid wood lipping glued on. The hinges should be substantial as they and their screws have to take the weight of a sitting person. Similarly, the shelf to which the stool is attached must be strong and securely jointed to the uprights at its ends.

There are ways of relieving the hinges of some of the load. A piece below the shelf edge will take the rear edge of the seat when down (FIG. 10-7D). And if the front support is set back from the edge of the top (FIG. 10-7E), its edge can rest against the top in the down position and take part of the weight. In the folded position this leaves a gap at the top, however.

A folding strut should be fitted to hold the front support of the seat upright and prevent unintentional closing. A ball catch holds the assembly up when folded.

11

Living Room Furniture

I N ROOMS USED DURING THE DAY, a combination of built-in and free-standing furniture works well. There is usually an accumulation of books, games, radio and television sets, and items for display. One use for built-in furniture is to provide storage for all these things and keep the room tidy.

In most rooms of reasonable size, chairs and tables are more convenient if movable. In a very small room it might be best to have a table that folds up to the wall, possibly with bench seats that fold with it. This would be especially appropriate in a dual-purpose room where a clear floor is desirable at times.

An office or study area is needed in any home. How elaborate this is depends on the work involved. If the home is large enough to devote a room to this purpose, it can be equipped as an efficient office; but in most homes only a part of a living room can be used, and some sort of a built-in is the best way of taking care of this requirement.

Furniture should be planned to match the decor of the room. There is a modern trend towards the severely plain. A purely functional unit that is little more than a block of shelves will fit into this sort of scheme. If other furniture in the room is traditional, antique, or colonial, some concession to this should be given in planning the built-in furniture. It

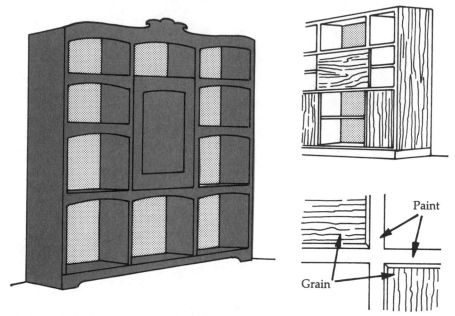

Fig. 11-1. Valuable storage space can be provided by a large wall unit, which can be given an ornate or severely plain finish to match other furniture.

might be possible to give the appearance of something from a bygone day by adding shaped or fretted pieces or including turned or carved parts. Still merely applying pieces that break up the severe outlines might be enough (FIG. 11-1A).

Much of the rather severe built-in furniture lends itself to construction in veneered manufactured boards. The attractive grain of the veneer breaks up the severity of the design. This is particularly so if panels are included that show their surface to the front. Veneered boards may form doors, drop fronts, or forward-and end-facing panels (FIG. 11-1B).

Shelves and other parts that only show their edges can be made of blockboard or particleboard without veneer and may be finished by painting. Even if there is no other paintwork on furniture in the room, a neutral or pastel shade will blend into most schemes (FIG. 11-1C).

WALL UNITS

Combined units that cover most of one wall are useful for multipurpose built-in furniture. Total needs should be assessed beforehand, as several different layouts might be possible. If you use solid wood available in sufficient lengths it might be simplest to carry horizontal lines right through (FIG. 11-2A).

Manufactured board is not usually available in lengths greater than 8 feet. This is usually more than enough for heights, but might not be

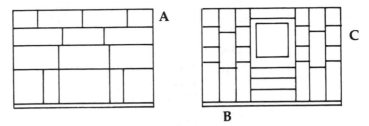

Fig. 11-2. For convenience in construction a large wall unit should be given shelves going right through, or uprights going right through, but not both.

enough to carry through the whole width. If you use this material it is best to carry vertical lines through (FIG. 11-2B).

Careful work will let lines in the opposite direction of the followed-through lines match, but the risk of slight discrepancies showing will be reduced if different sections are staggered (FIG. 11-2C).

Usually wall units project uniformly from the wall. This simplifies construction, as all parts are the same width. Breaking up the front line however, can improve appearance as well as provide better storage. For instance, a sewing machine might need more back-to-front space than other things, so a section of the wall unit may be made wider (FIG. 11-3A). This will also apply if a drop-front desk is built-in or a chair out of use is to be pushed under a desk (FIG. 11-3B). Alternatively, it might be better to reduce the width in cramped quarters where chairs have to be pushed under (FIG. 11-3C).

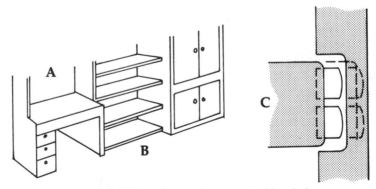

Fig. 11-3. Side units can be connected by shelves.

If horizontal lines are to follow through, the first parts made should be the shelves, base, and anything else that runs the full length. Mark these together so distances match. The only place where there might be slight deviations is in an end that comes against a wall at a corner. Check the wall with a level or plumb line. If it is out of vertical, allow for this when making the end parts.

Elsewhere in the unit, upright parts should be truly vertical, and not parallel with a faulty wall. Adjust the ends of horizontal parts accordingly. In an old house with very inaccurate walls, it might be neatest to recess a piece at the front to give a truly vertical start to the new work (FIG. 11-4A).

With the followed-through lines vertical, the method of construction will depend on the overall width. If this is little more than the height, the whole thing can be prefabricated, and there should be no difficulty in erecting and attaching the entire assembly satisfactorily.

If there is a large expanse of wall to be covered, it might be better to work in sections. Each section can then be treated separately (FIG. 11-4B). This does mean duplication of some uprights where the sections come together. Actually this double thickness can aid the appearance by emphasizing solidity. You could add molding over the joint, or just a strip with rounded edges (FIG. 11-4C).

A method of prefabricating of duplication is to make up alternatesections and add what comes between after these are in position (FIG. 11-4D). In this case, it is best for the more complicated parts to be in the prefabricated sections.

Much of the construction will be the same as described elsewhere in this book using dado, doweled, or manufactured joints for the main assembly. For shelves the joints can be permanent, which will help to stiffen the whole unit; but there are places such as bookshelves where height adjustments might be desirable.

There can also be metal strips that recess into the uprights and allow supports to be located in several places. Alternatively, there can be hooks

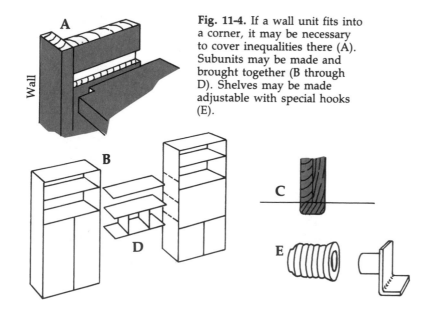

Fig. 11-4. If a wall unit fits into a corner, it may be necessary to cover inequalities there (A). Subunits may be made and brought together (B through D). Shelves may be made adjustable with special hooks (E).

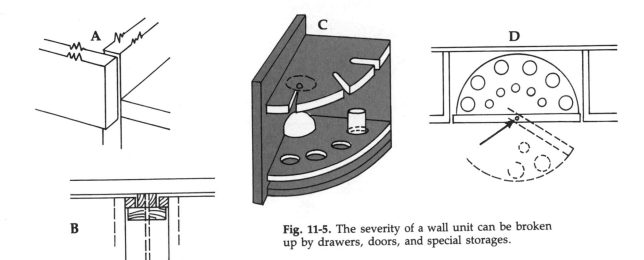

Fig. 11-5. The severity of a wall unit can be broken up by drawers, doors, and special storages.

on metal dowels that fit into holes in the wood or into plastic sockets (FIG. 11-4E). These may also be used for glass shelves, which then can be taken out for cleaning.

The front view is a multitude of crossing lines. This can be attractive, but if the line effect is to be reduced, doors and flaps can overlap the framework (FIG. 11-5A). This also applies to drawers (FIG. 11-5B) with the fronts hiding the runners.

If a cocktail or drink cabinet is included, this can be lined with formica and given glass shelves. Doors can accommodate glasses, either standing in racks or hung by their stems (FIG. 11-5C). The door may pivot centrally so everything housed there is brought to the front on semicircular racks (FIG. 11-5D).

DESKS AND STUDY CORNERS

The essential part of a desk is the worktop. Care should be taken in planning to make sure that this is big enough. Even if it is big enough, it can become cluttered and effectively reduced in size if adequate storage space for other things is not provided.

Also take into account the many things that will be associated with writing or typing. An L-shaped working top built into a corner is particularly practical. The typewriter comes around the corner, ready for typing yet out of the way of other desk work (FIG. 11-6A).

The working surface can be built permanently in place, possibly with shelves or drawers underneath as in many office desks, but fixed to a wall. You can give it an interesting appearance by sloping it back and

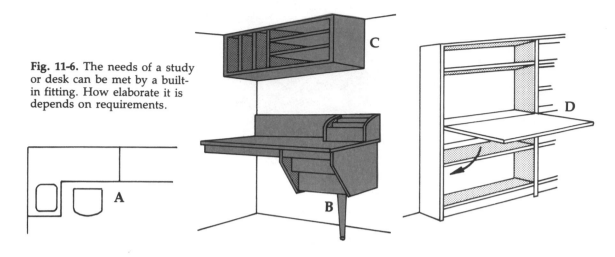

Fig. 11-6. The needs of a study or desk can be met by a built-in fitting. How elaborate it is depends on requirements.

adding a leg (FIG. 11-6B). Above the working surface there can be an independent wall unit (FIG. 11-6C).

The various things that accumulate on a desk might detract from the beauty of a room, so a flap front that closed over them is often a good idea. This can be arranged in one of the ways described for kitchen cabinet fronts in Chapter 8.

Sometimes it is best to have a front that folds downwards. This can be arranged in a simple shallow desk with bookshelves (FIG. 11-6D). The flap can have two or more hinges or a full-length piano hinge. Brackets can be hinged below (FIG. 11-7A), or a pair of frame legs something like those on a gate leg table can be added (FIG. 11-7B). The legs can be tenoned for maximum rigidity, which can be an advantage if the desk is used for work requiring steadiness.

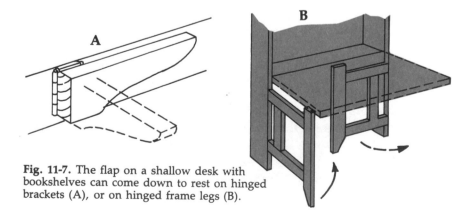

Fig. 11-7. The flap on a shallow desk with bookshelves can come down to rest on hinged brackets (A), or on hinged frame legs (B).

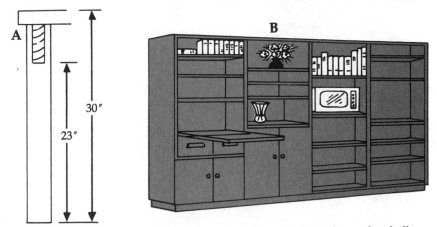

Fig. 11-8. To allow knee room, the drawer under a fixed top has to be shallow (A). The need for a workable home office unit might call for extensive construction (B).

Be sure to allow enough space at the back of the working surface for essentials. Things required close at hand, but not quite so often needed, should be given other accommodations. Bookshelves are nearly always needed. A drawer under the fixed top is valuable, but it should be shallow to allow for a comfortable surface height and knee room below (FIG. 11-8A).

Even when the desk does no more than provide space for dealing with household business, files are desirable. These can go in a deep drawer.

A home office unit may develop into a fairly extensive piece of furniture (FIG. 11-8B). If the desk is to form part of a living room, it should be given a good finish. Space can be allowed for things like displayed china, picture frames, and mirrors, which will soften a strictly formal business look.

A compact desk designed to rest against an open wall repeats the angle of the sloping front in the legs (FIG. 11-9A). The shelves reach the wall, but the feet are away from it. The flap can be supported by simple hinges with folding stays (FIG. 11-9B). Decorative veneering on the exposed front of the flap will enhance its appearance.

DESK CONSTRUCTION

Construction of the desks described can be done in the ways already described. There can be internal fittings to take papers, envelopes, and all the other paraphenalia that goes with office work. It is especially satisfying to make these parts using traditional methods. This involves working with fairly thin wood, which can be joined in several ways. Although the racks and pigeon holes could be built in, they might also be made as a unit to lift out (FIG. 11-10A).

If wood of sufficient width and no more than a ⅜-inch thickness can be obtained, the corners can be dovetails (FIG. 11-10B). If you are using

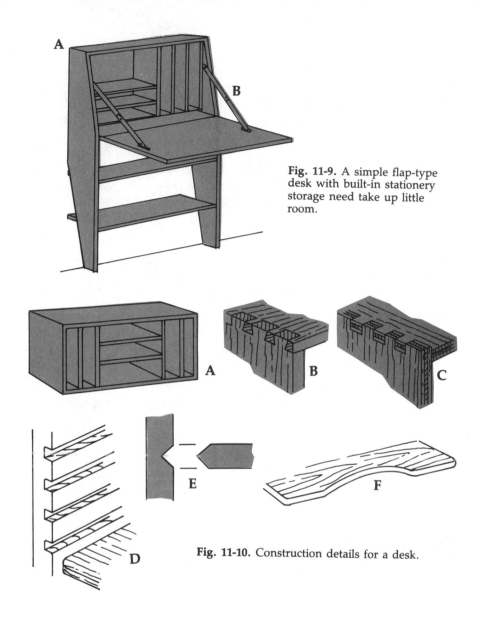

Fig. 11-9. A simple flap-type desk with built-in stationery storage need take up little room.

Fig. 11-10. Construction details for a desk.

plywood, comb joints may be better (FIG. 11-10C). Divisions can have dado joints.

If divisions are to be adjustable, make a large number of dado grooves so shelves can slide out and be changed (FIG. 11-10D). If the whole construction is to be fixed and all parts are thin, there will be less weakening if V notches (FIG. 11-10E) are used instead of dadoes. All front edges should be rounded, and there may be hollows cut for ease of gripping papers (FIG. 11-10F).

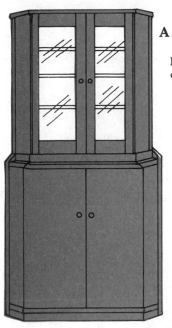

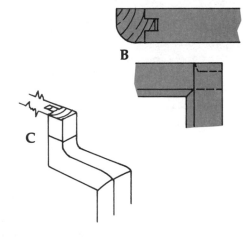

A

Fig. 11-11. The corner of a room is often wasted; a display cupboard there is attractive and useful.

B

C

CORNER FIXTURES

A corner is a good place for displaying china or trophies, so a glass-fronted cabinet is appropriate. The lower part may have a wooden door (FIG. 11-11A).

Although a traditional corner cupboard of this type would have been made of solid wood, this is probably best made today out of manufactured board with veneered faces and lipped edges of matching wood (FIG. 11-11B). The piece is shown with a step between the two levels, which necessitates a special joint in the lipping if you wish to avoid exposed end grain (FIG. 11-11C).

After the two main parts are lipped along their exposed edges, they are joined in the angle, and the other parts are made to fit between them. If the corner of the room is less than a right angle and the cupboard is made a right angle, the front will fit closely and the gap at the back will not show. If the corner is wider than a right angle, a gap at the front will show. Put the main parts in position and temporarily fasten them, then check the angle that will have to be used for the parts between them.

Wings extend from the main parts, and the doors hang on the wings. Shelves inside may reach the wings but should be cut back to give clearance to the doors (FIG. 11-12A). If glass shelves are used in the upper part they can rest on narrow battens or hooked studs (FIG. 11-12B). The glass-paneled doors should have tenoned joints to resist any tendency to flex and possibly break the glass. The glass is held by a rabbet with beads (FIG. 11-12C).

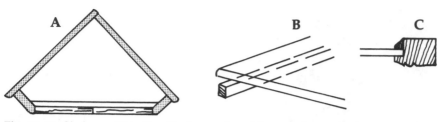

Fig. 11-12. Shelves within the display cupboard have to be cut back to clear the doors (A). If glass shelves are used, they can rest on batten (B). Tenoned joints in the doors (C) resist flexing.

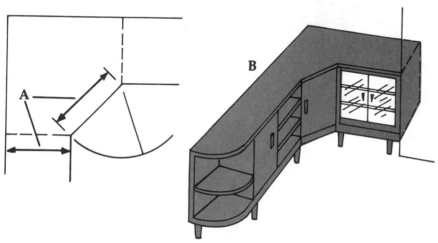

Fig. 11-13. In a corner assembly, access to the corner has to be considered, the feet have to be high enough for cleaning, and a member to tie parts together should be included.

If the usual manufactured board about ⅝ inch thick is used, the door framing should be about 1⅞ × ⅞ inch and the wings should be this size or slightly thicker to provide stiffness where they support the door hinges.

It is sometimes possible to extend a corner cabinet along one or both walls. The capacity of a corner cupboard with short wings is slight, but this increases as the wings become wider (or deeper). The door size is reduced, however. If there are extensions, you can enlarge the wings until they and the door are about the same width (FIG. 11-13A).

How the extensions are arranged depends on the room and the purpose. Such an assembly can often be made to accommodate a record player and its speakers. It can also serve as a sideboard or bookcase. If you have things that you would like to display, some of the doors can be sliding glass. A possible layout is shown in (FIG. 11-13B). Although there could be the usual plinth, this example is shown on short legs.

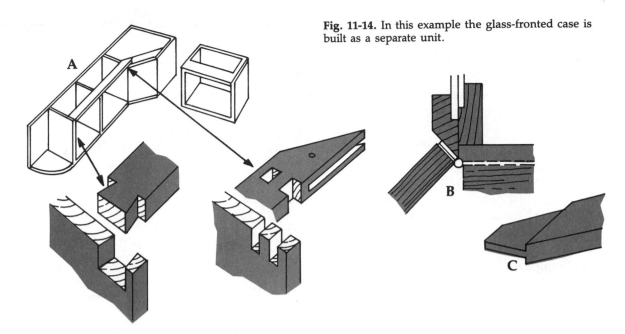

Fig. 11-14. In this example the glass-fronted case is built as a separate unit.

This sort of built-in furniture can be prefabricated in units—the corner and two separate extensions, or the corner as part of one side and the other extension separate (FIG. 11-14A). In any case, the top is best treated as a whole, and applied after the lower parts are fixed. The meeting parts of units can be faced with hardboard or plywood, providing front edges will be covered so as to hide this. A point to watch with a corner door and extensions is that there is sufficient clearance for the door to swing back without fouling. It is advisable to set back the extension on the hinge side slightly (FIG. 11-14B).

With this sort of assembly it is always good practice to arrange some of the structural parts to tie the assembly together. In the case of an extension-and-corner assembly, a front rail can either be recessed and screwed in place, or it can be dovetailed at its end. Double tenons can come at intermediate vertical parts. The strength can be carried around the corner with a bridle joint (FIG. 11-14C).

FOLDING TABLE

A built-in fixture can include a combination of table and benches sufficiently large to be used for meals. The space behind the folded parts can serve for storage of plates, cups, cutlery, and other things needed for the meal.

The method of folding and supporting the table and seats can be very similar to that shown for stools beside a fire (FIG. 10-7). Arranging parts so some weight is taken off the hinges is important, particularly for a heavy table or a seat for two or three.

The parts fold into a wall unit that is generally similar to one designed for books. The actual size of the table is governed by the height of the room. It will be used at about 30 inches from the floor, and its top should not be so long as to hit the ceiling when folded (FIG. 11-15A). The bench seats will be hinged lower, so they could be longer; but there is little advantage in them being more than a few inches longer than the table (FIG. 11-15B).

Getting the lengths in relation to the height of the room should be the first step in planning one of these units. Of course, additional wall width can be used for more storage space.

If the legs must be as close to the tops as possible when folded and there is no room for anything except the hinges, secure the legs to the floor in the down position with bolts (FIG. 11-15C). If a little more thickness when folded is acceptable, the benches and table can have narrow side pieces and folding metal struts of a type that lock in the down position (FIG. 11-15D).

You might want to include the option of tying the bench and table legs together when down, using a removable crossbar (FIG. 11-16A). This does not prevent accidental folding, but it links the three legs so they resist folding together. A removable strut can also be used diagonally between

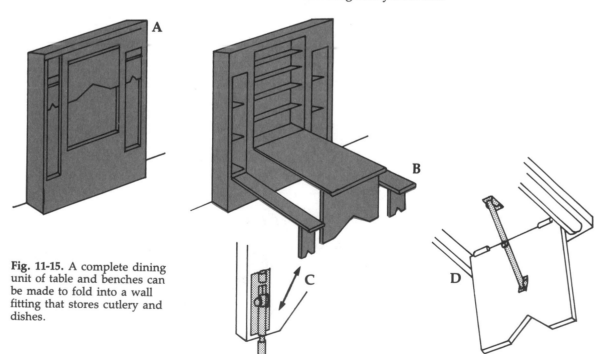

Fig. 11-15. A complete dining unit of table and benches can be made to fold into a wall fitting that stores cutlery and dishes.

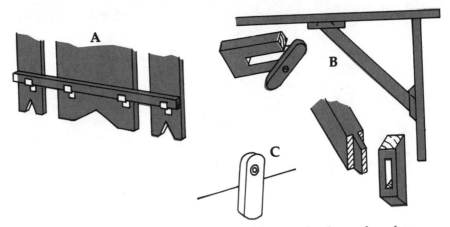

Fig. 11-16. Joining the table and bench legs with a crossbar keeps them from folding together (A). The tabletop, held by a strut to the leg when down (B), can be held up when not in use by a turnbutton (C).

the top and the leg. It can have a tenon at one end, but the other end will need a locating block and some sort of catch or a turnbutton (FIG. 11-16B).

The table, when folded up, needs a secure fastening. Bolts can be used, although fairly large wooden turnbuttons held by bolts are effective (FIG. 11-16C). Making them lopsided and loose on their bolts will ensure their dropping to the locked position by gravity.

12

Bedroom Furniture

A PROPOSED PIECE of built-in furniture has to be considered in relation to its ability to serve the uses intended. Functionalism can be checked by regarding the piece as a number of separate units. Hanging space in a clothes closet can be determined by measuring clothes on hangers. Drawer sizes can be determined by measuring what is to go into them. If washing facilities are to be included, stock sizes of tops and washbowls will give you unalterable dimensions to which adjoining parts have to be adjusted.

MULTIPLE UNIT

A great variety of multipurpose built-ins can be made by combining various units with different purposes. For instance, two clothes closets can be made, then a dressing table can be made as a shelf between them (FIG. 12-1A). Each closet may have a swinging door with a mirror inside (FIG. 12-1B). The whole width of the inside may be hanging space, with a shelf above and one or more drawers below (FIG. 12-1C). Drawers that come inside a door do not have space for a handle unless it is a folding one, but notching the drawer front provides a grip without projection.

If the closet is wide, the inside can be divided so that there is a block of shelves or small drawers at one side. Wide fronts can have double

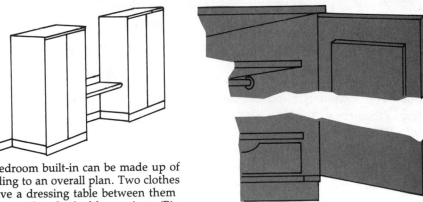

Fig. 12-1. A multipurpose bedroom built-in can be made up of several separate units according to an overall plan. Two clothes closets, for example, can have a dressing table between them (A); each could have a swinging door backed by a mirror (B). Options for the inside include a shelf and drawer (C).

doors, which are more convenient and project less when open. Sliding doors do not expose all the contents as swinging doors do, but they may have to be used where there is little space for swinging doors.

In a floor-to-ceiling arrangement in a room with a high ceiling, doors for the full height might be excessively tall. It is then convenient to have a cupboard above the clothes closet. The cupboard can be built into the same structure or it may be a separate unit. It could go across two closets (FIG. 12-2A). The doors should not be too wide, and the handles should be within reach.

In a small fitting the dressing table may be a single piece of veneered manufactured board, but you can improve the sturdiness by attaching stiffeners beneath the back and front (FIG. 12-2B). The front stiffener can be shaped to provide a knee hole (FIG. 12-2C). Alternatively, there may

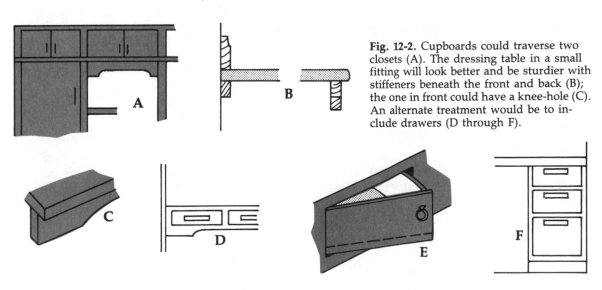

Fig. 12-2. Cupboards could traverse two closets (A). The dressing table in a small fitting will look better and be sturdier with stiffeners beneath the front and back (B); the one in front could have a knee-hole (C). An alternate treatment would be to include drawers (D through F).

be one or a pair of shallow drawers (FIG. 12-2D) or a swinging compartments for cosmetics (FIG. 12-2E). With a wide dressing-table top, there could be a block of drawers to the floor at one or both sides (FIG. 12-2F).

Embellishments

Such a combined unit will look rather plain at this stage. The appearance can be improved without additional construction by using contrasting colors. The drawers, doors, and tabletop could show the wood grain, and the trim and paneling could be painted.

Plainness can be broken up by several other devices. Large decorative handles may be used in a matching system for drawers and doors. This can be carried further by adding a pair of lamps inside the clothes closets and over the dressing table (FIG. 12-3A), preferably in a style that complements the handles. Another way is to apply moldings to the door fronts (FIG. 12-3B). The moldings could be painted to contrast with the doors; gold on a cream background would give a luxurious appearance.

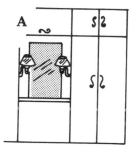 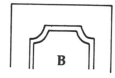

Fig. 12-3. Decorative touches for a bedroom unit.

A dressing-table mirror can be arranged in several ways. A square or shaped one can be fixed to the wall (FIG. 12-4A). It should be tall enough for people of various heights, either sitting or standing. The mirror can also be supported on adjustable fittings between two pillars on the dressing table, sufficiently far from the wall to allow adequate movement (FIG. 12-4B). The fittings could be on brackets projecting from the wall. A long mirror could have its fittings on the clothes closet sides (FIG. 12-4C).

The space between the clothes closets can be decorated by a cornice (FIG. 12-4D). It may have some sort of decoration, such as a carving, or it may hide a fluorescent lamp. You could also hang drapes from the cornice to the mirror (FIG. 12-4E).

Drapes can be very effective in breaking up plainness and integrating the new piece of furniture into the room, particularly if they match other hangings or bed coverings. The drapes could be arranged to draw to the sides, revealing a mirror or picture.

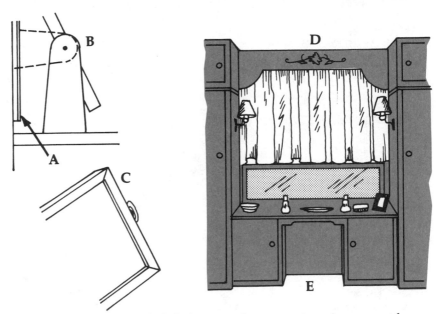

Fig. 12-4. If mirrors are included, they must have room to swing or must be arranged at a height to suit various users. The space over a mirror and dressing table can be decorated with drapes and a cornice.

Sliding Doors

A fitting in which sliding doors are appropriate and often essential, is a bedroom storage unit that runs the full width of one wall. This combines clothes closets, chests of drawers, hat shelves, and other storage units, all hidden behind doors. The number of doors depends on the overall width, but these should be about the same widths as the subunits enclosed. With two rails it is then possible to slide doors far enough to completely expose at least one subunit. With the inside divided into fourths and with four doors on two rails, it is possible to expose half the contents at a time.

For this sort of thing it is usually a good idea to make the interior as units, dividing the width of wall into convenient sizes. To avoid duplicating adjoining sides, alternate units can be completely prefabricated and positioned, then the intervening units can be fitted between them.

You could mount the sliding doors on the front of the fitted units, but it may be more convenient to keep the doors and their rails separate, mounting them under a wooden batten across the ceiling a short distance in front of the units.

SMALLER CLOSET

Clothes closets are necessarily large to serve their purpose. For two people the best arrangement usually is two closets arranged as just described.

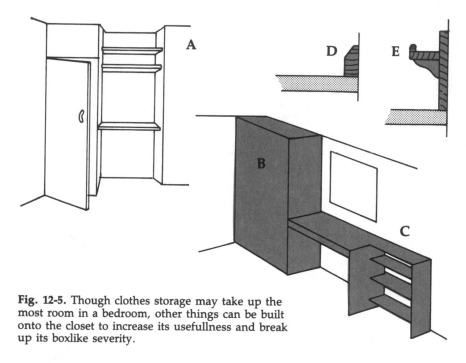

Fig. 12-5. Though clothes storage may take up the most room in a bedroom, other things can be built onto the closet to increase its usefullness and break up its boxlike severity.

If there is only one person's clothing to be accommodated, a more compact unit is possible.

If space is limited, the whole thing can fit into a recess (FIG. 12-5A). Against a straight wall the clothes closet can be arranged in the corner, where its size will be less obtrusive (FIG. 12-5B). The dressing-table top can extend into a bookcase (FIG. 12-5C).

Where a tabletop comes against a wall, something should be done to prevent damage to the wall covering. A strip of wood on edge might be all that is required (FIG. 12-5D) or there may be a higher piece carrying a shelf (FIG. 12-5E). Where the working area has a washbowl set in, the top and any protection behind it can be plastic, and this can extend a short distance down the front.

Construction Details

Any of the methods described earlier in the book can be used. You could use veneered manufactured board, but for large areas it can be expensive. An alternative is to build up a framework for the major units, with members at places where shelves and drawers will come, then cover the framework with plywood or hardboard. Pairs of end frames can be made up complete and joined with other parts (FIG. 12-6A).

The covering may overlap at corners (FIG. 12-6B). Mitering there for the length of a joint might result in slight discrepancies that will be more

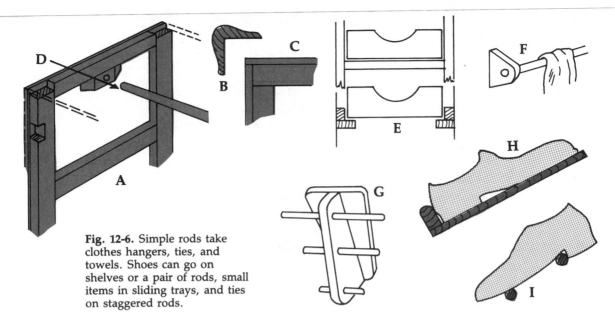

Fig. 12-6. Simple rods take clothes hangers, ties, and towels. Shoes can go on shelves or a pair of rods, small items in sliding trays, and ties on staggered rods.

apparent than the narrow overlap. Corners can be covered with molding (FIG. 12-6C). Backs and tops may be hardboard or plywood if the wall surface itself is unsuitable at the back of a closet. Any storage place for clothing should be dustproof, so a back as part of the furniture is desirable.

Various types of rails to take clothes hangers can be bought. Quite a simple rail is a dowel or metal tube with its ends in blocks (FIG. 12-6D). If the rail has to be removed, one end may be in a U-shaped socket instead of a plain hole.

A block of small drawers or trays will accommodate small dress items and jewelry. It is possible to use plastic or metal trays intended for office filing. Similar trays can be made from wood. They can fit close like ordinary drawers, but it is convenient to provide them with runners and allow spaces between them (FIG. 12-6E).

Ties, belts, ribbons, and similar items might be better hung on a rail, which could be inside a door. This could be a wooden or metal rod between supports (FIG. 12-6F) or staggered rods projecting from a central support (FIG. 12-6G).

Shoes and other footwear can go at the bottom of a clothes closet or in a shoe cupboard on the end. If there is sufficient depth for suitable shelves, the shoes can lie flat. This arrangement will take the greatest number of shoes in a particular area, but it means a shelf width of at least 12 inches. If this much cannot be allowed there can be sloping shelves with ledges to hold the shoes (FIG. 12-6H) with the heels downwards. Shoes will take up slightly less space if arranged the other way, either with the shelf cut back to allow heels to hook over the edge or with a pair of dowel rods (FIG. 12-6I).

CORNER DRESSING TABLE

In small bedrooms consider the use of corners. In some arrangements there might be a little waste space in the point of the triangle, but this will be compensated for inconvenience. A dressing-table mirror can come across the corner. It need not necessarily be at 45 degrees (FIG. 12-7A). If it is arranged at another angle, there could be some advantage in the use of limited light or space.

If you use a corner assembly, you must accept limitations of drawer shape and capacity. The dresser can have a front with the corners at right angles to the walls, then drawers can be taken as deep as the shape will allow (FIG. 12-7B), narrow drawers going deeper than wide ones. If the corner is other than a right angle, the possible depth of a drawer becomes less, although this can be increased if the back of the drawer is cut on a slant (FIG. 12-7C).

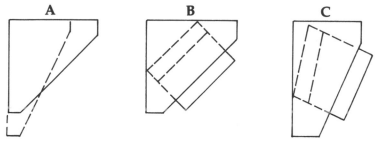

Fig. 12-7. A corner dressing table need not make a 45° angle with the walls (A). Drawers have to be arranged to make best use of the unusual geometry involved (B and C).

Check the angle of the room corner and make either the actual top or a template to match. Never assume that the corner is truly a right angle.

If the dresser is to be removable, it can have a plywood back. Otherwise there need only be sufficient framing to support drawer guides and take screws that fasten into the wall. If there is a base molding in the room, you can cut it back, or cut the dressing table to fit over it (FIG. 12-8A). It might also be possible to have the plinth at the same height as the base molding. It can follow the shape of the front or can be taken straight across (FIG. 12-8B).

The angular vertical joints at the fronts can be mitered and glued. Blocks can be glued in the angles, but if the joints are accurately cut and fitted, sufficient stiffening will probably be provided by drawer rails and other framing carried across these angles (FIG. 12-8C). Be careful to make the

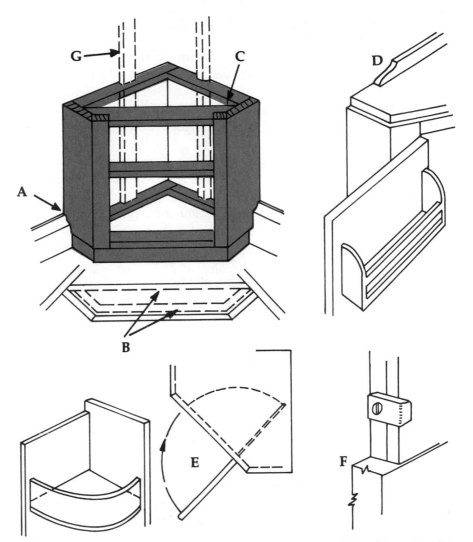

Fig. 12-8. Making furniture to fit a corner brings some special problems, but this dressing table takes up minimum space. It may be given drawers or doors.

drawer guides at right angles to the front. The drawers are made in the usual way and can be fitted between the framing or arranged with overlapping fronts.

If you want maximum capacity, use doors instead of drawers. Whether to have one or two doors depends on the situation. The doors will swing back to the wall, and it is possible to fit racks or shelves inside to take toilet items, cosmetics, etc. (FIG. 12-8D).

If maximum capacity is not of prime importance, you can arrange curved shelf blocks on the doors (FIG. 12-8E). Transparent plastic sheets bent around the curved shelves will keep stored things in place yet allow them to be seen when needed.

A mirror in a corner cannot be designed to tilt, so the common swinging arrangement cannot be used. This means that the mirror should be fairly tall to suit users of various heights and allow a full-length view. Its lower edge may rest on the top surround (FIG. 12-8F). The mirror is clipped to a piece of plywood screwed to uprights, which are carried down the carcass to provide stiffness (FIG. 12-8G).

Because its triangular shape makes work on the table more difficult than with a rectangular piece of furniture, it is best to construct the table in its entirety before affixing it to the wall. You might need to make several trial fittings as work progresses. Complete all but the painting or polishing before screwing the dressing table in place.

BOOKCASE HEADBOARD

A bookcase fitting can be made to go over one or a pair of beds, with one or more shelves or a built-in electric light over a single bed (FIG. 12-9A). Individual lights can be built in over twin beds and the fitting can be brought down between the beds to provide a table (FIG. 12-9B). The bookcase need not project more than about 5 inches and will not interfere with movement in the room.

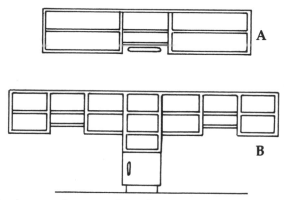

Fig. 12-9. A bookcase makes a good headboard fitting. It may be cut back to take a reading lamp or extend to the floor between two beds.

If you are making the fitting from solid wood, corners can be dovetailed, rabbeted, or doweled (FIG. 12-10A). Shelves may be extended to allow for dado joints (FIG. 12-10B). There could be an open back so the wall covering shows through, but it is probably better to use a plywood or hardboard back recessed into rabbets (FIG. 12-10C).

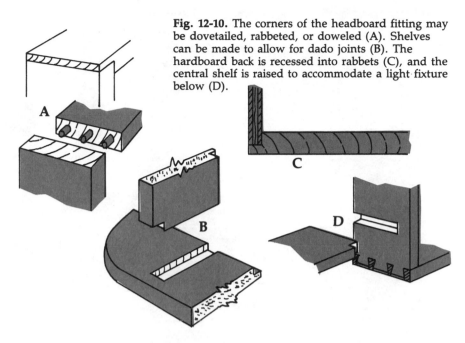

Fig. 12-10. The corners of the headboard fitting may be dovetailed, rabbeted, or doweled (A). Shelves can be made to allow for dado joints (B). The hardboard back is recessed into rabbets (C), and the central shelf is raised to accommodate a light fixture below (D).

The light fixture may come under the straight bottom shelf, but it and your head will be protected from knocks if the central part of the shelf is raised a few inches (FIG. 12-10D).

Books are fairly heavy, so attachment to the wall should be strong. The load is best taken by screws to the wall near the top, with a few fastenings lower to keep the bookcase close to the wall. A strip across the back and under the top can take the load-bearing screws, or drilled metal plates can be arranged below the top. If the back is thin plywood or hardboard, screwing directly through that without something to transfer the strain to structural parts might not be sufficient.

CHILD'S BOOKCASE HEADBOARD

In a child's bedroom there is a need for a place where drawings, cutouts, and pinups can be temporarily affixed. A child might not have many books to house, so the headboard bookcase can be adapted to provide a pinboard, a display shelf, and limited book space (FIG. 12-11A).

For construction you can use either manufactured board or solid wood. A piece of plywood might do for the pinboard, but pins are easier to push into soft boards made for that purpose. There can be a different material behind a shelf (FIG. 12-11B). This need not be the full thickness of the pinboard if it is built up at the lower edge (FIG. 12-11C).

If the unit is more than about 3 feet long, one or more dividers (FIG. 12-11D) should be fitted to prevent warping of the shelves and help

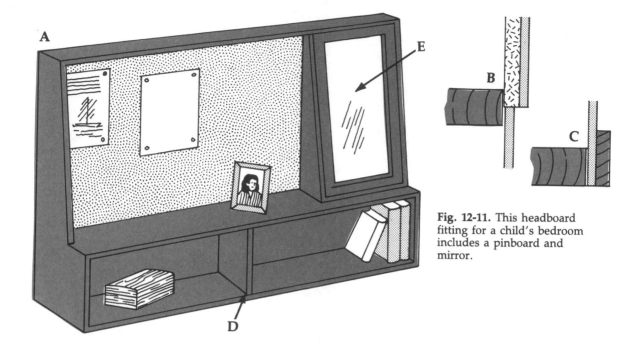

Fig. 12-11. This headboard fitting for a child's bedroom includes a pinboard and mirror.

support books. You can add storage shelves on each side of the pinboard, or there can be a mirror at one end (FIG. 12-11E).

High Storage

If there is enough head room to allow a cabinet at ceiling height, construction is straightforward. Remember that loads will come on the unsupported bottom, so plan your work accordingly. If you can arrange the length so the assembly fits in a recess, both ends can be attached to the walls, and most of the load will be taken there. If one end can come in a corner, that end should be firmly attached to the wall. Elsewhere, arrange structural parts to resist pulling apart so that the load will be transferred to the wall or ceiling. Metal or wooden shelf brackets can be put below to supplement the fastenings through the back.

Vertical members should overlap horizontal members if you use nails, screws, or dowels for joints (FIG. 12-12A). These joints resist side thrusts better than they resist pulling apart. The strongest joints are made with dovetails with the tails in the upright parts and the pins in the horizontal parts (FIG. 12-12B). Covering the structure with plywood, fixed with glue and pins, helps to consolidate the structure and resist any tendency for parts to sag or break away (FIG. 12-12C).

The strongest attachments can be made high at the back. Next strongest are those at the ceiling, and then lower fastenings.

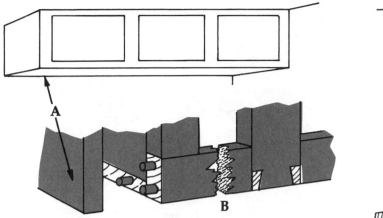

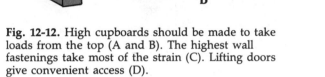

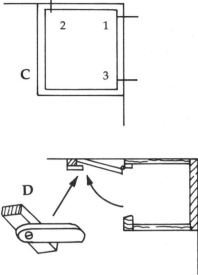

Fig. 12-12. High cupboards should be made to take loads from the top (A and B). The highest wall fastenings take most of the strain (C). Lifting doors give convenient access (D).

How the doors are arranged depends on the use and position of the fitting. The doors may be hinged vertically, but they will probably require handles fairly low so they can be reached from the floor.

Use sliding doors if there is little room for swinging doors. In some circumstances it might be better for the doors to swing upwards (FIG. 12-12D). A turnbutton on the ceiling can hold a door up.

Index

Edited by Joanne M. Slike